MW01600181

Printed in the United States of America

ISBN: 9798671667370 (paperback)

LCCN: 2020915401

Categories: Nonfiction / Poetry / Anthologies

Cover design and art copyright © 2020 by Ben C. Ward

First edition: December 1, 2020

PERSPECTIVE

TO

PEN

An Anthology

Edited by Ben C. Ward

Created by Robert A. Cozzi

CONTENTS

INTRODUCTION

Akin to many collaborations, this anthology was born from a simple conversation. Fellow anthology poet Anthony Rivera and I were on an Instagram Live broadcast when a viewer asked if we had any plans to collaborate. That simple question spawned an energetic conversation that became *Perspective to Pen*, a poetry anthology lovingly put together by people who love to write words for the people who love to read them.

Twelve talented poets showcase voices and styles as diverse as they are. Being of many various ages, genders, races, orientations, and nationalities, each poet joins together here to create a work greater than the sum of its parts. This anthology is focused on sharing and exploring a plethora of differing perspectives, becoming separate yet simultaneously united. Throughout these pages, you will find multifaceted expansions on very human experiences, like the ecstasy of a first love, the treacherous pits of loneliness, raw and crippling grief, the visceral beauty of nature, the nostalgia of childhood, just to name a few.

I welcome you to grab a pen and write in the margins. Circle your favorite words, highlight or underline the lines and verses that speak to you the most. Dogear the pages you wish to revisit and, most of all, read between our lines. Imagine yourself beyond the words.

On behalf of the poets featured in this anthology, I'd like to thank you for purchasing a copy. All proceeds from this book's sales support Amnesty International's continued and critical battle for human rights. Before the book begins, there are poems written by each poet dedicated to Amnesty International and their mission.

Thank you for taking a stand with us.

–Robert A. Cozzi

This anthology is dedicated to the freedom of speech, the strength of words, and the fortitude it takes to stand behind them.

At The Ready

My sisters!
My brothers!
Your beautiful voices are stolen
by those who lock you away.
My ears bleed at the news;
rage sets my heart ablaze.

Raising my voice, I answer the clarion call.
Ancestors!
Poets!
Warriors of light!
Join us in this battle,
join the righteous fight.

Marching into darkness, our voices loud and steady,
we prepare for battle, pens at the ready.
United, we sing till truth drowns out lies,
until we need no longer shout
and a whisper will suffice.

-Lisa Bain

Those Silent Ones, Destined to Speak

The weight
Of all your unspoken words
Must be unbearable

Your voices deserve to be heard
And we are not stopping
Until they are all set free

We know that this obstacle
Appears insurmountable
But just remember this,
Everything that is silent
Is destined to explode
So, once your voices have been unleashed
Tell the story of who you are and what you love
Refuse to be erased
It matters
You matter

-*Robert A. Cozzi*

Seeds

The titans have been released,
the Uighurs in their mouths
and the bones of Syrian mothers
clutched as weapons to beat
migrants and protectors,
students and seekers of justice.
They're making spears from
the homes of displaced people,
Rohingya and Venezuelans,
poaching the great beasts,
our evolutionary brothers.
Our graves have been dug
and our weak bodies chucked in
where we are expected to decay.
The poet Christianopolous
told us what we are,
that we are seeds and burying us
is how we are encouraged to grow.
We treated him like Cassandra
had been treated, ignoring him.
Still, I've seen new leaves
bursting from the sides
of the limp bodies.
I've watched hope take root.

-Brian Fuchs

A Place for Peace of a Human Right

Centuries of fight of grief, of strife.
Lives lost within the battle for life,
Freedom cries for nations to gather their young
To huddle them close, no preferences for one.
Humane they fought for voice and fairness
We solute those heroes that have passed on, fearless.
This, our baton we must carry now
To solidify a place
For peace
A human right.

-Shanika Benoit

The Shield of Justice

In a world where man's armor is based on status,
the country you grew up in,
or who your parents are/were.
Where money is holy and justice an afterthought
We stand united for those crippled by society
For if you don't have a sword to fight back let us be your
shield.

-*Max Asbeek Brusse*

Worlds Apart, We Stand Together

Worlds apart
Humans pulled apart
As power mongers climb bank ledgers
Never maxed out
Down we go
Heels on skulls
Oppressed
Compressed by the ones we expect to lead justly
We won't be silent
Our voices of international magnitude echo through
Have you heard of *Horton hears a Who?*
That's exactly what we do
Together, we shout
"We are here! We are here!"
We stand together, magnifying efforts
No matter how small
A voice that is united cannot be forgotten
And if it's ignored - we will join hands, too
Together we demand humanity with relentless unity
The oppressors fear us
Call us treasonous
Trying to divide us
Only to hear
"We are here! We are here!"
And we will never back down

-Emily Salt

Many People Are Afraid

Of the dark
Trauma causes them to lock away
and seal up all their heart
Struggle tears apart
The Hope living in their thoughts
One candlelight
Defeats the might
Of those that cause the strife
Across the earth
They do the work
Changing course of life
Reproductive rights
Working on an app to save your life
Imagine being jailed
Just because you toast to something right
They've given more than fifty years
Even Helped Mandela
Then he became a peer
International
Never over rational
Bringing amnesty to all
Efforts we can all applaud

-*Anthony James Rivera*

Amnesty or Death

Yesterday I turned on the TV,
And came face-to-face with death.
A starving mother and child,
Oppressed for their beliefs.
The subjugation men and women under tyrannical rule.
Free speech postponed, and lives taken cheaply.
The groans of their voices eclipsed by the growl of their
empty stomachs.
Buck broken men turned to little boys,
Turned out for the price of their expression.
Carcasses littered in roads amongst,
The toll of epidemics and brutal regimes.
Watching as I ask, "What's the price of a human life?"
When two men cannot express their love?
When children are bought and sold as chattel,
As the spoils of warring tribes?
When a lack of faith belies a faithless system?
Where cultures clash in conflict?
Where the indigenous are the expendable?
It was then that I saw a naked flame in the darkness.
Those willing to stretch out their hands,
To give light to those who need it most and hope to those in
doubt.
To show them our compassion.
Complimented with our love.

-Nathaniel Chin

Locked Arms

stand next to me brother
lean against me sister
locked arms
human beings
dreaming throughout the night
all fighting for the same light
hold my hand brother
grab on tight sister
locked arms
minds dancing
souls swirling
locked arms.

-Cody James

Letters to Anonymous Pt. 6

Dear Anonymous,

No one else can feel

Like the person you are.

Hindering yourself from

The recognition you deserve

Is poisoning your image,

Even if you're hiding it.

Nowadays, a voice that speaks the truth

Is more powerful

Than any household name.

Promise me you'll never forget

That face in the mirror.

Forever & Always,

-Davian Williams

War

Mighty men march holding
Self-righteous arms–
Quick, sound the alarms!
Forgotten foreign names
Flash faster than bullet speed.
Under hot heavy suns,
Million pounds of frightened flesh
Boil into distant dreams.
Broken bones of old & young,
Fathers' smashed skulls
Mothers' shattered souls
Hunted down without a trace
Under Holiness in vain.
Hell on Earth is wherever a war.
Humanity's heavenly plead:
Man need not one more!
Man need not one more!

-Carl Straut-Collard

Battleground

It is the time, without question.
Unite, for there is no other solution.
The cries amplify through the smoke and the ringing
is all too clear. The shockwave has left.
I hear a mother's voice, cracked but not shattered, crying out
in prayer for her child whose eyes never used to look
so sunken.
There are those who survived the bombs dropped and
boldly face an uncertain life. They will not be destroyed.
They will not be ruined.
What are the walls? A conduit for courage, calling for a
demonstration. There will be no defeats as long as
there are dreamers.
A Vietnam veteran stands prominently in front of the line
of soldiers, grizzled, worn, but unceasingly unbroken.
The young blood sprays him straight in the eyes and stalks
onward, cold and unforgiving.
The police have shot yet another unarmed black person.
Why must we say, "yet another one?"
It is the pandemic before the pandemic.
We must forge new measures of peace, from the fires of love,
compassion, and empathy.
There will be no rest.
There will be no submission.
Signs are our shields and protests are our swords
on this international battleground.
The world's future is upon us, here and now.
Come,
let us fight for it.

-Ben C. Ward

PERSPECTIVE

TO

PEN

An Anthology

Lisa Bain

Lisa Bain became a young widow in 2016 after losing her husband to cancer. She quickly learned we live in a grief-phobic society that isolates the grieving even further. The Idaho-based author took off on a (nearly) two-year solo trip around the globe to work through the grief process and found her voice along the way. With both humor and heartbreak, she incorporates grief and bereavement issues into her keynotes, blog, poetry (featured in Ireland-based Poethead), and her debut novel, *Heart of a Kingdom* (The Light Network, 2019).

Her poems are snapshots of love, death, and the journey of starting over. Sometimes they rhyme. For more, visit: TheRealLisaBain.com or on Instagram @LisaBainWrites. For all other muggle and magic shenanigans across social media, check out @TheRealLisaBain.

Butterflies

I'm fully submerged; a blanket of bubbles pulled up to my lazy smile. Belting out Butterfly, off-key and at the top of my lungs, is justified since I have this wing to myself, and it's only late afternoon.

I didn't hear you until you were already in my room. I'd forgotten to lock the door.

Jumping up, I slosh water and bubbles all over the marble tile. Crazy Town is still singing in my airpods.

The look on your face is a blend of "I'm gonna get fired" and "best Friday ever." You stammer your bit about the complimentary bottle of wine from hotel management in your limited English. I'm sure it's flawless when you don't have a bubble covered American standing in a pool of water.

When I finally regain my senses and reach for a towel, you hastily turn and leave. I can feel you grinning as my cheeks burn, and I lock the door.

Butterflies Part 2

It's the off-season in Dubrovnik, which is why I splurge on the five-star resort. The deal is too good to pass up. It's also why the smaller crew is working every shift.

I walk into breakfast alone to be greeted with the smell of fresh coffee and American-style bacon. I haven't seen American-style bacon since I left home six months ago. For a split second, it makes me hungry and nostalgic.

And then I notice the heads turn, and every one of your colleagues is suddenly grinning like a schoolboy.

Before I know it, you appear at my table, still wearing that grin I gave you yesterday You're now my waiter. Great. I want the floor to swallow me up. But not until after I've had some coffee.

And bacon.

The soundtrack to my departure is a burst of laughter from the kitchen. I can't help but join in as my cheeks burn once again.

Believer

Dedicated to Ryan Wallace, The Opera Guy of Belfast

I await your arrival with eager anticipation. My mind wanders back to that dreich day I first heard you singing in Belfast. You, so dapper, and your angelic voice delivering messages from heaven, right there in the middle of Cornmarket.

Has it really been three years?

Today, as you begin to sing my favorite song, Bocelli's version of Fall On Me, the hazel eyes smiling back at me suddenly belong to another. Just like the first time we met.

They say angels walk among us. You make me a willing believer.

Zoom Life

Together in our isolation,
we share our beauty.
In our separate closets of night,
we stitch together light and color.
Creating life;
sending it out over the ether
to weave us together
in a patchwork cocoon of the brightest love.

Stirling Silver

It's late morning on a weekday, and the café isn't full. But when you see me dining alone, you choose the table across from me, situating yourself so we're facing each other. I have a sudden image of us as Victorians at a ten-foot table, and a giggle sneaks out. I accept the initial greeting you lob over the space between us.

I mentally squeal when you call me lassie in that soft brogue and check it off my list of Scottish experiences. It feels fatherly. You kind of remind me of my dad, and I resist the urge to hug you.

You listen so intently when I share my travel stories. You're easy to talk to, and when you ask me why I'm on my own, I can't hold the words back. My recent widowhood spills out over my lips against my will.

Your kindness spares me the look of pity I've come to despise. And my heart can tell you know it all too well. It's why we're both dining alone.

Stirling Silver Part II

Dedicated to Richard McDonald, the piper of Stirling Castle

We talk about music, something we both love in a way only the bereaved know. I take notes and write down all your suggestions. You invite me to hear you play the bagpipes at Stirling Castle tomorrow afternoon, but I am booked on the early train to Oban. I suddenly want to change my plans so I can spend more time with you.

And then you burst into song, right there in the middle of Our Place Café. You serenade me with Wild Mountain Thyme, reminding me to write down the Joan Baez version in my fancy phone. I feel other patrons looking at us, but I only see you.

The smile on your face mirrors the one in my heart. You allow me to take your photo, provided I email it to your son. He helps you with your computer.

The rough wool tweed of your coat scratches my cheek as I hug you goodbye. I dash out the door before you see the tear escape my eye.

Bilingual Maybes

you did a double take when you caught me staring
but held my blushing gaze
no spoken words exchanged
in your smile, we explore the future
before time resumes its normal course
and releases us from a bold, bilingual maybe

Music Lovers

I walk into the pub late and you're already on stage.

You begin to sing that song; the one you put on the playlist you made for me. You won't make eye contact, but I feel you watching me as I order my drink.

When you sing the last word, your mouth turns up at the corners and you finally look at me. You catch me running my fingertips over my bruised lips at the memory of your kisses and I blush as you fail to control the desire on your face.

Hurricane Ophelia

The wind screams through the chimney as Ophelia settles in over Killarney. You are my only friend here. Or were, until we had a fight two days ago. That should have been the end of it. But you know I'm here alone, and your better nature kicks in.

You brave the hurricane to show up at my door, peace offering in hand. I'm not especially nice about it, but the wind carries my harsh words away and we sit in awkward silence in the front room. I look over the rim of my whiskey glass at you in silence. You fidget like a naughty student sent to the principal's office but meet the storm swirling in my eyes.

When the wind and rain die down, we walk arm-in-arm into town. The storm blew away the anger and memories of why we fought. You laugh at me as I try my first Guinness. I roll my eyes as you complain (again) about my expensive whiskey taste. We laugh and dance and drink it all away. The music sets the night ablaze and the smoke from a turf fire hitches a ride home in my hair.

Baggage (v. 2)

Heaving my suitcase onto the bed
I drop it on the floor instead,
Oops, forgot it's full of laments for my dead.
Why did I pack the weight of grief and fear
when all I want to do is be light and clear?
Running away and starting over is my plan
So why did I decide to bring along a dead man?
I silently berate myself, forcing tears away
Someday I'll acknowledge what it took to make it to this
day.
But for now, unzipping my bag, I dump the contents on the
floor
I'm done with this.
I refuse to carry deadweight with me anymore.

Exposed

After checking my seatbelt for the seventh time, I look
around to distract myself from my usual take-off jitters.
Your bare ankle catches my attention from across the aisle. I
avert my gaze as I wonder why I feel my face flush in
embarrassment.

My eyes can't stay away from the naked skin between your
trouser hem and shoe. So bizarrely intimate.

A wave of vulnerability crashes over my heart as a random
memory of my hand, resting sleepily on the warm skin of
another ankle, surfaces. I shake it off, returning to you and
cruising altitude.

As small as this plane is, I could reach across the aisle and
touch it. I want to. Instead, I hold my drink with both hands,
looking out the window at the clouds below as my palms
daydream about the feel of your skin and memories melt
into maybes.

Ancient Echoes

I join my sisters in a circle around this old cold henge.
The druid in our midst calls forth ancient echoes from the
towering stones,
rooting us deep in the Earth and across time.
Hands clasped, electric, in this ancient prayer of light,
the hair on the back of my neck stands
and I weep as the sun sets fire to night.

Home Again

I secure the coveted perch next to the window. Closing my eyes, I bask in the warmth of the sun on my face. My brain generously overlays a beach track, and the sounds of lapping waves replace the hustle and bustle of the crowded airport.

Childhood memories leap to fill in the gaps and I take flight. Warm, powdery, sand slowly squishes between my toes as I walk along the liminal edge. My efforts to avoid stepping on the LEGO-sharp pinecones are distracted by the view of Na Mokulua and the sun glinting off the too blue to be true water. I breathe deep the elixir of coconut oil, salty air, and barbecue. The lazy breeze picks up the lilting sing-song melody of the islands, wrapping me in the magic of home.

At least until final boarding call for the giant bird taking me even further away.

Grounded

when all movement stops and forced stillness begins
there's nowhere for a nomad to go but within
no boarding pass needed, no suitcase to check
no passport, no visa, no vaccine requirement

solitude prepared me for this dive in the shadows
who i'll emerge, only the universe knows
this wasn't my choice, but i'm done running away
what better use is there for a quarantine day

Robert A. Cozzi

Award-winning poet Robert A. Cozzi continues to dazzle his international following with poetry and prose that tantalize all five senses and leave the reader wanting more. In addition to five published poetry volumes and inclusion in anthologies and publications, the New Jersey-based writer also shares daily creations and livestreams on Instagram.

Educated at James Madison University and New York University, Cozzi shares valuable mentorship with new writers around the globe. He was also the creative force behind assembling this anthology.

Cozzi is also featured in the poetry anthology "Social Distances" (2020, Scissortail Press) and was a featured poet three times over in The World Poetry Movement's publications, including "The Best Poems and Poets of 2011."

Also by Robert A. Cozzi:
tide pool of words (2013, Beach Umbrella Publishing)
Handful of Memories (2014, Beach Umbrella Publishing)
Blanket of Hearts (2016, Beach Umbrella Publishing)
Sky of Dreams (2018, Beach Umbrella Publishing)
kaleidoscope of colors (2019, Beach Umbrella Publishing)

For more, visit RobertCozziAuthor.com, on Instagram @RobertCozziAuthor, and on Twitter @RobertACozzi1

Dark Velvet

I walk along the sea
As dusk pales to twilight
My shadow, so apparent in the day
Evaporates into the obscurity of the night

I scan the outermost reaches of the inky Atlantic
Watching the stars blink and wink in the water
Looking as far as I can
To the place where the sky touches down

I hold my gaze on that spot
Until I see you
Until I see us

The purr of the sea
Becomes far away and unreal
Like its echo from a shell
Slackened to a slower rhythm we understand
A rhythm we have created

New Years' Eve 1997

It was the first New Year's Day in New York
That I could remember being unseasonably warm
The sky was cloudless and endless
As I stared up from your rooftop garden on Greene Street
In the heart of SoHo

You stood next to me
And in our silence
We spoke to each other
Keenly aware of the other's quiet movements
We breathed in tandem
Our eyes
Were full of hope
Lingering on that infinite blue sky
Unaware that one of us would leave this world for good
In the ending days of that September

Only Me, Only You

I love
How we fall so easily
Into this cadence we create
Your eyes,
      The dusky promise
            Of a long summer
My eyes,
      Glassy
            Like a still pool of water
Deferring intruders
      From its depths
            By distracting them
With our reflections

One More Chapter

I sit in your white Adirondack chair
Because it makes me feel closer to you

The African violet you left behind
Is thriving out here, one year later
You would love that

Above the roar of the surf
I hear the opening chords of "Sara"
Coming from the radio inside
I turn, tilting my ear to the music
And I hear your voice being played back too
It is hollow and distant
Like an echo from another time
But I recognize the timbre of your tone

Then, as if on queue
The wind picks up
Just as Stevie sings, "And the wind became crazy"
And I just smile, knowing that this is one more chapter
In a story
No one else
Will ever believe

Elijah

The first time I saw you
Was not in the video
Of you being murdered by the police
It was in the video of you on your birthday
Smiling that bright smile, as you walked in the door,
surprised
I remember thinking to myself as I watched, "No, God,
please not him!"

I have been trying to write about you for weeks now
But the words have not fallen onto my pages easily
Because I am still angry
Why would anyone want to hurt you?
I cannot wrap my head around any of this

The more I read about you, the more I see your soul
From the images of you playing your violin for the lonely
kittens
To the way your eyes shine, radiating love and purity
You were unique and different
It is obvious that you lead with kindness
A quality so rare these days

Being different got you killed, though
And I will never be able to accept that

I am still reading about you when I fall asleep atop the
covers
Beside me the blue green lava lamp burns, and the Stevie
Nicks song

"Has Anyone Ever Written Anything for You" plays low on
the radio
I dream I am you
Fighting my way through an inky blackness
To a surface
To light, to air
It is not a frantic, drowning feeling
It is slow and warm
Like I am being asphyxiated with precision

Maybe this is how it felt when they injected you with
Ketamine

As you, I struggle and strive to attain freedom
So I can find peace
But when I finally burst out of the dark
The world I see
Is so traumatizing
That my eyes snap open
My lungs gasp for air

I hope your experience
Exiting the darkness was different from mine, Elijah
I hope you found peace in the bright lights of a new world
One where differences are embraced, and love abounds

Down here, we will never forget you
Down here, we will fight for others like you
Fight until the brutality ends
Because anything less is simply unacceptable

October 2, 1997

The day I return to your loft
It is unseasonably hot

Once I arrive
I sit on the stairs
Listening to the buzz of the city

It makes me feel hotter

Your rooftop garden
Cautions me from above
Between us stands the old oak tree we sprawled under
reading Kerouac
It ridicules me with its silent serenity

Time passes slowly
At various junctures, I consider moving
But I sit here for a half an hour
Before eventually stepping back onto the pavement

I size up your building
Feeling oddly like it is something to overcome
For the first time ever
I feel like I am trespassing

A window in your living room
Catches my attention
I begin wondering
If I have seen something move
But the sun reflects so brilliantly on the glass as I squint into
the light

I realize that I could not have seen anything behind the
brightness

Inside your loft
The air is not as heavy
One of the polaroid's I had taken of you is on the kitchen
table
In it you are making a peace sign with your fingers
I put the photo in my pocket

Beside the bed you never made
I find your copy of *On the Road*
I flip through it, remembering when we first read it together
Under the shade of that tall oak tree

That day seems so long ago now

Under the bed
I find the journal I gave you for your birthday
The one filled with your last written words
I flip through its overflowing pages
Penned in your distinctive loopy handwriting
Suddenly, I am weeping
Salty tears stain my cheeks and slip into my mouth
Before falling onto the open pages
I clutch the journal to my chest
And kneel before your empty, disheveled bed

The emphatic sounds from the ticking clocks
Bounce off the walls
They come back to me from all directions
Attacking
Pummeling

And mocking me
I seize them all
Beating them, pounding them on the stone floor
Smashing each one until there is no hope for repair
When I am done, my breathing is as heavy
As my heart

Living Alone in 2020

Sometimes
Music is his only comfort
Brokenhearted lovers mourning their losses
Lamenting their loneliness
Is all that salves him
The music brings the sting of isolation
To such a precise agony
That it makes him feel less alone

He sings along with the passion of the bereft
But when the music stops
He no longer can think
Of a way to quell
The echoing silence

The Sound Heard Above the City

It takes a moment for you
To look up from the book you are reading
You are seated at a small, stained-glass table in this intimate
outdoor café
An array of emotion fills your face
Before you stand up, with your inherent grace
You still have a swimmer's build
But your eyes are not as blue
They seem to have faded gently, like a memory
Your hair is no longer tousled and bleached from the sun
It has matured into a darker, more conservative looking
blonde
When you come to me, we embrace
A grimace of happiness cracks my mouth
As a veil of your aroma envelopes me
Bringing back the feeling, not just the memory
Of the years we spent together
Inside this embrace, I can feel the sand of Folly Beach
And smell the ocean air and remember what it was like
To be so completely loved by you
But once you pull away
I hear my heart crack above the sounds of the city

Pausing Summer

We make cheeseburgers in the kitchen
Because the evening is too brisk to grill outside
I stand watch over the sizzling meat
As you slice the cheese and tomatoes
A firefly crawls up the window screen
Flashing on, off, on, off
Outside, the wind violates the slumber of the leaves
Bringing with it the sober reminder of fall
A flicker of worry, like heat lightning, passes through me
I tap on the counter to the beat of the Prince song playing
To dispel any sense of doom
Noticing this, you take my hand, pulling me to your side
I nestle my face in your hair
Breathing deeply your scent
It is salty and clean
Like the summer I wish I could pause

"Thanks for Loving Me so Much"

Sometimes what travels forward comes back
This is what happened to me today
When I pulled mom's copy of *Essays of E.B. White*
The one she gave to me right before I moved to South
Carolina
From the shelf of my bookcase

When I open this volume from 1977
Several old *The New Yorker* magazine clippings pop out
Each one written about E.B. White
Mom always kept such things in her books

I turn to page 157, where my favorite essay,
"Afternoon of an American Boy," resides
And I am surprised to see
A handwritten message from you
In the top margin
A message you wrote 22 years ago
A message I have never seen before that reads,
"Thanks for loving me so much."
Followed by a heart drawn in pencil

It is not all that surprising
To find something from you in the margins of one of my
books
Because this is something you did often
Sometimes you would leave your thoughts in the margins
About the meaning of things
Other times you would just circle the words you loved
Or highlight lines you wanted me to read again

Most often, though, you would write something to me in the
margins

As I stare silently
At your distinctive, Catholic school cursive letters
Everything else on page 157 moves backward in a blur
As if time is rewinding
Back to when the world was some other place

The familiar image
Of you sitting
At my kitchen counter on a stool
Heels hooked on the bottom rung
Elbows on knees
Book in hands
Completely focused
And not at all fazed by
The sea breeze from the open window
That shifts your golden blonde hair around
Passes before my eyes
In silent lucidity

Suddenly
I reach for my phone and tap your name
You answer on the third ring
In your trademark southern drawl

Quickly, I tell you of my discovery in the margins
My words spill out rapidly
My mind tells me to slow down and pace my words
But my heart has other plans
When I finish, I hear silence on the other end
Until you respond with, "Wow, Rob, just wow!"

I recognize the catch in your throat

I love how much this affects you too, even after all these
years

You tell me that you remember writing this
The night before you left Charleston for Savannah
You wanted to be sure I never forgot how much it meant
To be loved so completely

Prior to hanging up, you tell me you love me
It is something we still do
Each time we talk

A platonic love is what we share these days
But each time I hear you speak those three words
My senses turn on
Oxygen prickles in my lungs
Making it seem as though
I have been living in a black and white film
That has suddenly been draped in Technicolor

How We Used to Be

Remember when
We'd stay up late at night
In our dusty little beach town
Breathing in the salt air
While lying on top of your car
Holding hands
Staring at the stars above
That twinkled with hope and uncertainty
Just like us?

Do you ever think about us on star filled nights?
Or when you breathe in the salt air?
And do you dream about how we used to be?

You probably don't, though
Because it's been twenty years we've been apart
And you've been married for eighteen of them

I know you're happy with him
But sometimes I wish you weren't

Walking the Tightrope

The thought that you might actually love me
Forms like a tightrope under my feet
The thin line
Dangerous and selfish
May not be thick enough to hold us both
But will you still choose to tread across it with me?

Chuck's Roof

Your garage roof
Was pitched and perfect for star gazing

The stars that draped the summer sky
Were as big and low as lanterns

We'd lie side by side
Gazing up
Talking for hours

We felt everything so deeply

The world around us
Was accelerated and intensified

I am thankful we had each other
And for the comforting knots of teenage platonic love
That kept us from ever feeling alone
Or unloved

Packaged Words

When you died
I packaged up your words
And hid them for later

Whenever I feel alone
I open them up
And let them break me back open

June 30, 2006

The last day of June
Is heavy and sticky
It makes us lazy
We kiss for hours, until we know nothing else
The intimacy is a bit overwhelming
It heightens my senses of smell, taste, and touch
I am not even sure if the salt I taste on your lips is sweat or
the sea
In bed, we lie together
Me behind you, my head resting on your shoulder
One leg nudging between yours
This is always how we sleep
To me, it feels like home
The contours of our bodies fit
Like ridges and valleys
Your sparseness meets my fullness
As if we had broken apart and, separate, were incongruous
But together, we are unspoiled and perfect

BRIAN FUCHS

Brian Fuchs was raised by a family of educators and has lived in both Oklahoma and Alaska. He is inspired by the venation of insect wings, by the wrinkles he remembers on his grandma's hands, and by the poetry of James Schuyler, Frank O'Hara, Ron Padgett. Brian is the author of several books of poetry including *Okie Dokie* and *Scissor-tailed Flycatcher* and *Muskox vs. Unicorn*. He currently lives and works in a bit of forest that runs through northern Oklahoma.

For more information about Brian and his work, visit him at brianfuchs.com.

The Day Roxie Died

Mom and I talked about new artists,
the ones we wanted to emulate:
Karla Morreira,
Margaret Organ-Kean,
Paul Klee.
We tried to pull them from ourselves,
to put ourselves in their minds,
mused about allowing ourselves
the freedom of expression,
the courage to let the brush reveal.
The paint was a song,
cardinals at dawn,
vireos at dusk,
geese in formation.
It greeted us cheerily, harshly,
excitedly.
I showed her a piece I loved,
a watercolor by Organ-Kean
of a beautiful woman,
of a moment I started to remember.
The colors pooled,
grains settling into a gradient,
an ombré of white flesh,
amethyst-colored beads,
auburn hair.
A lakeside landscape sprawled out
in purples and greens
beyond the edges,
whispers and suggestions,

hints of willow trees
lazily swaying along the lake's shore.
I could hear the marsh wrens
and the cinnamon teals
just out of view.
I'd never be so disciplined,
never let the absences themselves
tell the story.
Mom was focused on flowers,
trying to find their forms in her hands.
They would appear,
frustrate her.
She wanted to be surprised,
to find flowers she hadn't already seen,
but they bloomed on the page
just as they were in her mind.
Dad was on the phone,
crying with cousins I didn't know
as we painted,
our efforts a memorial
even before we'd learned the news.
I didn't know Roxie,
her colors were pooled
in the suggestions,
the whispers,
in the moments I wanted to remember,
ombrés of Dad's childhood,
portamentos, melodies, footnotes,
Clovis,
Artesia,
Lubbock,

the Atchison, Topeka and Santa Fe,
cattle and watercolor skies,
the music of hummingbirds,
throats saturated with amethyst,
pigments and dyes,
notes and tones.
We kept painting,
our heaviness coaxing from us
romantic abstractions,
loose landscapes,
spontaneous petals.
Our memories felt real,
transformed and shaded,
and we all felt the absence
and the clarity of a wren
as it began to sing.

Confessing to the Epimeliads

I can still see him
bursting from my belly,
back to Mary's arms,
reverse through the abattoir.
I'm dry-heaving in distress
as his blood is returned,
as my crimes are put right.
Somewhere he's healing,
sutures fading
where his baby body
has been sewn together,
where his bones are once again
holding in the soft flesh.
Flocks had passed before,
dissolved in my hideous gut,
their names unknown to me.
Even now I fail to see them.
The heaving continues,
my body still full of guilt,
of sinew and muscle,
photos of family
posing with the lifeless corpses
of cousins and siblings.
When I've finished heaving,
when the last scraps have gone,
when I've at last turned away,
exiling myself,
I'll plant apologetic clover
and pray for his forgiveness.

Eight Minutes in May

I'm just a yokel,
nothin' in my noggin 'cept dust
while old fires burn,
when souls cry out
to finally be heard,
when hearts have all exploded
over the same pavement
where their necks were pressed
and lives snuffed out.
The police are suiting up for combat,
firing up the tanks,
readying for war,
and I'm still standing in place,
slack-jawed,
shocked,
tears filling my face.
I feel my neck pressed
on the pavement,
imagination squeezing out my life,
filling my pores with a rage
I didn't know was possible.
Only imagination,
no knee holding me down.
Only imagination,
no onlookers witnessing my death.
They did this
You did this.
We did this.
I did this.

My legs are frozen;
the march goes forward,
tear gas rushing through me.
People are rising,
beautiful and triumphant.
People are lifting their voices,
earnest and finally
at the end of their rope.
I'm projecting through space,
climbing my family tree,
finding ancestors
and preparing the tree
where they deserve to dangle,
where their necks should feel
that rough jute rope
as my ghost hands grip,
slip the noose and let their
useless lives slip away,
unnoticed and unremarkable.
I'm no price to pay at all
if they'd never existed,
and beauty was left to flower
in traditions and families
who never deserved abuse.
The police are marching on our streets,
storming our homes,
taking us out before we get a good look,
before we see their monsters.
Fires are burning.
People are rising,
bodies engulfed,

effigies of collective esophagi.
No air gets through.
The nurses fight through rubber bullets,
clad in medical-grade garbage,
supplies looted and spilled.
The nurses fight,
shove tubes down our throats.
Now none of us can breathe.
Everything is burning.
Our lives are burning.
Our lives mean nothing.
The floodgates must be torn down;
let the flood of melanin
wash over everything,
drown us, the children of terrorist.
They did this
You did this.
We did this.
I did this.
I'm starting to close my mouth,
my esophagus is catching fire.
I'll either breath the fire of my indignation
or find myself intubated,
a machine replacing my lungs.
It's only June,
and already the very air is burning
my skin. It's only been two weeks,
but it feels like 400 years.
The shock has faded,
rage shoots out
of my mouth in great bursts,

flame and smoke.
The police are locking arms,
demanding our submission,
demanding our allegiance,
demanding our loyalty,
blindness.
Let the pavement
'ever be pressed to our necks
so we can
never forget.

Helianthus annuus

For Annie

The sun is shining
through the spaces,
beyond clouds and skies,
the chattering of sparrows.
We were blooming,
opening up together
in a world filled with optimism.
We are all
the children,
the field mice,
the tethered kites,
the lazy swallowtails
drifting over a sea of yellow faces.
I'm lost in the flowers,
looking up toward the sun,
following it as it moves across the sky.
You are there too,
in the sun,
in tiny mouse noses,
in the laughter of children flying kites,
in butterfly wings,
following along with me,
your bright face next to mine.
We saw the storms,
looked through them.
The sun is always shining
beyond the clouds.

You are a field of flowers
as beautiful as my mama.
The sparrows are happy today,
and so am I.

The Stride of a Confident Woman

This was once her town.
I've moved through this place,
outside of my body,
through the soil and the trunks of trees.
It's never fit me the way it had fit her.
I've let my bare feet touch the heat
of an August sidewalk,
let the pain teach me lessons
about God and about life's meaning.
She was a mountain,
piled with the best of ourselves,
and she walked like our expectations
were the air beneath her feet.
She was carried by her confidence
above everything.
I used to study the way
she moved her feet.
I was a child in awe;
each hip announced itself,
entering rooms separately,
beautifully.
She was magic.
We all felt a crushing weight
and the sudden absence of might
when she died.
We were all left in the sun
without the shade of her smile,
the shelter of her hips
the grace of her stride.

We melted on the sidewalk,
seeped into the ground,
into the leaves of trees,
trees filled with mourning doves,
each one cooing a eulogy.
The halls of our church felt so empty
without her hips to fill them,
and downtown they built a garden,
lined with nandina and redbuds
where the doves can return,
remind us with their sad words.
I'm always learning to walk,
searching my legs for her gait,
her rhythm,
for a reason for bird eulogies.
I'm looking at other people
on what were once her streets —
people who never knew her,
who forgot,
whose lives have just started.
None of us are mountains.

A Mood

Mom can't cope.
It's been two years
and she feels lost,
abandoned.
Ambien & wine,
meditation,
vodka — well,
at least it's low-calorie.
She's spending time
figuring things out,
getting help with grief.
We aren't drinkers.
It wasn't what she thought
and her mom is still dead.
Everything smells —
mildew and potatoes.
It's old, everything is old.
I'm tired.
Mom can't cope,
and neither can I.
There's a new nephew
on the way,
only days away,
only a world away.
We need a distraction.
I feel nothing.
My brain is stuck in a loop,
replaying events,
phone calls,

conversations,
ultrasounds,
emergencies.
My friends all seem to be
bursting with advice —
all gibberish and platitudes,
misunderstandings and
well-meaning nonsense.
JoBeth is sick again. Cancer.
We've been through enough.
I want to kill myself,
but I don't want to die.
I want to disappear,
to fade into the atmosphere.
I'm thinking about John
lying in the hospital,
crammed in a casket
while the family ignored Ray,
who should've been his husband.
They didn't mention his name,
eulogized him without
acknowledging John
in all the ways he was John.
How could they ignore Ray?
My mind is numb.
I miss Mom,
and she's still here.
She's taking time to herself,
time to break from the vodka.
Everything is unraveling,
springing suddenly out of control.

My nephew will be here soon.
Maybe we'll all feel whole again,
maybe we'll all
just fade away.

SHANIKA BENOIT

Shanika Benoit is a Trinidadian-born poet, wife, and mother of four living in Connecticut. Shanika likes to write about love, self-reflection and general musings on life. Her work has been previously published in *Poetica Volume 1*, another Instagram anthology. Shanika is currently working on self-publishing her first poetry book, which you can look out for January 2021.

Her work can be found on Instagram @shanikajbpoetry.

When Shanika is not writing she is on her yoga mat or running and she loves having wine with family and friends!

Connect with Shanika on other platforms:
Facebook: @shanikajbpoetry
Twitter: @shanikajpoetry

Changes

I can only go through so many evolutions.
The heart wants what it wants, they say,
and my heart wants change.
A yearning, a pulling to become
an entity that seems to be beyond my grasp,
I can see her,
in her fullness
capable.
She's there tending to her needs
in preparation of becoming,
gathering all her thoughts,
energy.
allies.
Pregnant with ideas to birth
prepared for the labor and
willing to take on the sacrifice.
I see her
I can feel her
I am becoming her.

Loving for the Last Time

This is it.
we've touched for the last time,
and my body still carries the memory of you.
It echoes when the breeze caresses my skin
I feel you.
We've kissed,
a thousand times and even though
your lips no longer meet mine,
at night, I feel them linger warmly, softly
in my dreams, I think.
My thoughts are always on you
as if you were by my side,
I ask questions, waiting for a response,
and even though we are miles apart
I keep telling myself,
before I pick up the phone…
I'll be loving you this time,
For the last time.

Heart Ache

Like that bittersweet pain,
after a rigorous workout,
the kind that makes you
feel built and taut …. the muscles
have really just awakened
and you go at it again.

Like that sore feeling you get,
after a lustful night of lovemaking,
again and again…

that's how my heart aches after you…
I keep at you time after time
despite the heart ache.

On Guidance

It can arrive in a dream,
little nudges from your destiny,
a calling, a journey you must take.
It can come to you through people,
guides on your journey, a helping hand
they appear as thoughts, out of the blue
as they say...
When you look to the sky with questions
for direction
It comes from that little voice within
telling you, it is ok. It is time.
You are ready.

Demystifying Death

If only I can see beyond the veil.
To the narrative of the unseen,
naked, but not to our eyes.

Cloaked in a life fully living,
breathing not a necessity… existential bliss
no polarities.
Just be

surrounded by lush greenery,
colors abound and
scents not needed as
our senses are for only beauty,
A rhythm.

A rhythm unlike any other,
caught in a frequency that spans
time and place,
bleeding onto our existence,
in this realm we call
Earth.

Empty Feelings

Today I'll scribble
all the thoughts that I can possibly
put together
the sum of everything I've ever felt
when I think of you,
and I'll come up with
nothing.

A Journal Entry

Journaling my heart
a love lost, but not forgotten
a self left on the shelf
full of dust, never dusted off.

Passion written without
poetic form.
raw, open, unhindered
hopes and visions in
dreams.

Anger, frustrations and all It's unpacking...
letters,
oh! letters,
words weighted with feelings
all written in my heart.

Love, in the Making

I'm in the mood for you.
Yes, I've said it.
I will not deny this strong
urgency, that is my need to be close to you.

So close, the hairs on my skin
respond like an antenna in proximity
to a magnetic field

So near to you, that
your very breath warms the
cool of my skin... beneath my shirt

So on you, that
we blend like watercolors in an
artist's collage...
Yes, I said that.

This is love,
in love
making.

I Remember

When I felt like something
was missing.
When there seemed to be a piece
left out of the puzzle.
I was happy, yet not content,
living life,
a life, but not mine.

Waiting for something
or someone,
knowing that vibration is becoming
stronger with time,
even through heartbreak and grief
I remember ... knowing.

That it will all fall into place -
what I was waiting for
will, find its way to me.
That familiar.
That flame.
That part of me that was missing.
I remember.

No Labels

Free flowing, continuous
like the stars in the sky, limitless.
Uncontainable.
Just free.

Open, pure, full of hope and dreams.
overflowing.
joyous.
contagious and enigmatic.
Just let it be.

Sweet. simple. innocent.
Capturing the beauty of lifetimes.
Alluring. sensual. exotic....
wanting yet admiring the unknown.
It will be.

Lifetimes of loving, sharing
loss and grief,
slowly vibrates in the memory of
our souls.
The connection is undeniable.
unmistakable. irreversible.
and cannot be labelled.

Soulmates

What is this?
This feeling of sheer joy!
Like the innocence of childhood,
nothing matters but playing and
making new friends ...
the sun shines and you run out to
play,
The rain falls and you go out to play in
the rain.
Even when you are sad, you easily break into
a smile.

I see you, but I've known you
for eternity, it seems,
I've found my friend.
I saw you, and I knew you,
no words were spoken, but
my soul remembered our
conversations.

What is this?
This feeling of finding your way
after being lost...
of anticipation at opening a precious gift.
What is this... feeling?
Like finding your long lost
Friend.

Time Traveler

The only thing constant is change,
they say.
Everything changes.
but what is it about change that makes
time seem to stop?

Time as relevant to the traveler,
as leaves fall to the ground.
Yet through this change
our soul remains ...

Through centuries and seasons,
we've lost our memory
of the passions and pride,
love and wanderlust,
that would take us through the
winds of change.

Learning, growing, evolving...
To capture the essence of our
times lived.

Our memory doesn't change
that imprint of our lives,
the one thing that makes
Time seem to stop.

Of all the beauties in life,
Let the love of self,
The love for another,
The love from another,
Be the beauty you behold.

The end.

Max Asbeek Brusse

I am Max Asbeek Brusse, 23 years old, and I am from a small village in The Netherlands. Let me tell you a bit about myself. I grew up with a lot of bedtime stories. My mum and dad valued literature and thought it be wise to start early with me and my sister. Especially the Grimm's fairytales and all the Disney stories were their favorites.

Because all these stories took place in an imaginary world, my imagination was stimulated from a young age. Around the time I was 12 years old, I wanted to learn how to play the guitar. I picked it up quickly and around 15 years old I liked to create my own songs. I started to write my own lyrics and music. This was the beginning of my writing hobby. After a while, the songwriting didn't quite fulfill my needs anymore on a creative level; I needed something else. This is when I discovered poetry. I saw a movie where a poetry book of Charles Bukowski was displayed and fell in love. I was already fascinated by all the sayings we have in Dutch and wordplays. Since I have always been able to express myself in English, I started writing my poetry in English. First, it started with little poems or just some thoughts I had in mind.

Then I started a blog with completely random topics. I was interested in quite a broad pool of things, so I wanted my writing to display that. My blogposts were informative with a twist of humor—one quality I valued very much. I want my writing to have something light and imaginative. Because of my childhood I like to write in much detail. Whenever I am describing an emotion, an object, or a situation. Every piece of the image has to be right. So whenever the reader reads my piece, it provides scope for the imagination.

Thank you in advance for reading my pieces, I hope you can relate or if not at least giggle a bit. Yours sincerely,
The left handed writer.

Instagram: @the_left_handed_writer

The left handed writer

Sugar Rush

It starts in the morning
I wake up, brush my teeth, change my underwear,
wash my face and drink some water from the tab, leaving
my lips wet.
There aren't really breaks, you know, when you're doing
this professionally.
The mouthwatering starts around 5 min after I've woken up.
I haven't even eaten breakfast yet,
My whole body is already screaming, begging, aching to
receive some sugar;
just like a baby, who starts crying harder when
misunderstood.
You continue to ignore the urges and eat something plain
trying to restrain yourself from getting tempted.
But *just* like a baby, to make it stop crying, you have to put
something in their mouth eventually, cause let's be honest,
you can only last so long mentally.
The feeling subdues, but it doesn't solve the origin of the
problem. So we keep on denying the root of the issue and
start looking forward for yet another temporary high.

The First Time

I had this image in mind
To make it something memorable
To do it with someone I knew, loved, respected.
Before getting deflowered, to really have gone through all
the stages.
But you can only plan so much, right or not, we're creatures
of lust and once that flame is ignited there's few who can
extinguish its heat. So at 2 a.m. in St. Andrews, New
Brunswick, Canada. In an abandoned children's
playground; for obvious reasons.
Surrounded by walls of what probably was world's smallest
castle, I blossomed.

Comfort in the Chaos

Children scream
Drunkards howl away at the person sitting next to them,
not that they're actually listening, but only because they're
conveniently there.
The sound of breaking glass, shattering across the floor and
a server who's picking up the pieces.
"PING, PING, PING," the sign of the kitchen bell ringing,
meaning the dishes are ready.
The smell of stress and impatience is in the air, as I spot
multiple faces in the crowd throwing face expressions of
disgust and contempt at the waiters.
But I, I only have eyes for the tab in front of me and the
bartender, who's preparing the cold brewed beverage of
delight in a tall glass.
You see, these people working here, they're me; most days
of the week. But you have no idea what relief and what
amount of relaxation it gives me to be on the other side for a
change. I find comfort in the chaos.

Drifting Away

I paddle to the middle of the lake
Long strokes, making the water "slush, slush" around me.
Besides the company of some ducks I am all alone.
I rest my eyes and lie down in the boat.
My thoughts are buzzing; like a swarm of bees at their hive.
It makes me restless, but the silence helps.
The mist that's surrounding me gets thicker.
I am pretty sure no one at the edge of the lake can even see me.
Where the silence gives comfort it also feels like a double-edged sword.
My want and need are entangled.
Where the fog and silence feel like a warm blanket, my thoughts keep rudely awakening me from the dreamy state I try to enter.
At last I find the focus to occupy my mind with one thought
And I slowly, deeply, drift away…

Backpack of Emotions

Every journey brings you something different
Some are dull, some rich of adventure, and well, some are a
bit of both
But they are never quite the same.
You meet new friends, discover new places
Share stories, have a laugh and make new memories.
You'll feel joy, disappointment, excitement and boredom.
A rollercoaster of emotions.
All you can do is fasten your seatbelt and enjoy the ride.

The Polish Stewardess

It was midnight at a hotel in Paris.
I had just come back from a day at the fair.
We all gathered around the bar for a drink.
When we had one or two beers a group of Polish flight
attendants walked in,
all looking very elegant in their uniforms.
Some immediately went upstairs to their rooms,
but the others stayed behind for a drink at the bar.
My colleague, a mid-thirties married man. Tried to convince
me for his sake to chat up with the woman at the bar.
"Do it for me please, you see, I would hit on them, but this
ring around my finger and certain promises I made, prevent
me from straying down this path, you're young, you got
this."
I don't know why I suddenly felt compelled to prove a
point, but I pitied him, that his marriage wasn't as much fun
as he had anticipated. So there I went.

There were 3 young woman, mid-twenties. One blonde and
two brunettes.
Not that that detail matters, since I really don't have a
preference between either, but just to give you an image.
Their English was rusty at best, which made it hard for me
to connect with them, since my humor is my strong suit.
All that was left was my charisma and manly presence to
impress them, so you can understand I didn't really feel like
I had a leg to stand on.
For some reason that didn't matter, we got into various
subjects and actually had fun.
Time flew and it was 3 a.m. My colleague had left me 2
hours ago and had went to bed.

One of the brunettes was tired and had gone upstairs. So I was left with the two women.

From my time with them I had already noticed that the brunette didn't have any interest in me; also, she was very distant and short with her answers.

This told me she probably had a boyfriend and that she stayed around because she didn't want to go upstairs by herself. The blonde suggested I came up to her room and so we did.

Like the freaking 3 musketeers we laid next to each other. The brunette, clearly now cockblocking me, started to say to her friend that she should send me away because SHE wanted to sleep. I knew she stayed in a different room, so her suggestion made zero sense. Me, who had already put in way too much time effort was kind of getting frustrated that it took so long. I decided to get more dominant and made the brunette go away so I'd be alone with the one woman I did have a physical attraction to.

We were lying in bed and she then started to tell me a story that she's only had sex with older men. Mainly because she'd been let down in the experience by earlier attempts from men with a similar age as mine. I obviously told her I was different, but she was not convinced. From the stories I told her what my reason was for being in Paris. She told me, "If you're such a salesman, sell me this bottle of water. If you convince me, I'll let you go down on me." Hold up, back up a second. This must've been the weirdest request I've ever received to prove my skills in the bedroom. I was so incredibly tired, but somehow my sex drive had sustained the adrenaline rushing through my body and so I did what she asked of me. To be honest it wasn't that hard because she was already into me, horny and slightly influenced by the drinks we had earlier. This however didn't faze her at all, because, well, she was Polish, so if I have to believe the stereotype, she was in way better shape than me. Conveniently enough the item I had to sell was a bottle of water. More precisely a bottle that was cold from the mini bar, and quite lengthy if I say so myself. I decided to get a little bit Mr. Gray action in there. But instead of the ice cube I used a bottle. It was a simple one + one equation.

It already looked like a shaft so why not remind her that instead of this cold plastic thing, she could have something in the flesh. After teasing her intimate parts with an Evian water bottle, she budged. We then threw one another around the hotel room for about an hour till our adrenaline wore off and we basically passed out. Till this day I don't even remember what her name was, but I do know one thing. That night was freaking legendary.

Believe

We struggle and we fall
We tumble and we crawl
We look up and declare
What has given us despair
We trace our steps and look at our mistakes
We then realize what's responsible for our mental breaks
Our confidence was wounded
And our spirit tested
The cure right there, but our hearts infested.
We run past the solution and avoid the door
That leads to our salvation, all those restless nights, no more.
Another day arrives and the tides are turned
Another day survived another lesson learned.

The Bench

It's not so much that it's comfort
or the gentle breeze that's passing by
It's a place for people to come and go.
A place to rest, a place to think.
A beacon, a lighthouse, a landmark that guides us on our
way.
A reminder that you don't always have to go forward,
but can stay a little while and enjoy the moment.
Until time sweeps you off your feet again and the moment
walks away.

The Tracks of a Generation

Round and round it goes
The same distance every time
We think our tracks aren't laid out for us, that we have a
choice in the matter.
How naïve we are.
Our parents, the government, universities, institutions.
Unless they cease to exist, we all have certain tracks laid out
in front of us, made by the ones who went before us.
Our opinions, thought processes, arguments, why we are
who we are and where we're headed.
All seem to feel like a whole lot of nothing if you start to
question why you "chose" to do what you've done for the
first 20 years of your life.

Poem for a Girl

Hazelnut brown eyes, living in paradise.
Cutie with a smile that leaves you wonder for a while.
In summer she drinks slush puppy on a daily, with a
rainbow of colors matching her crazy.
She's into rock and roll, not the modern shit, *that* she finds
dull.
She's a busy bee,
Being a nurse and making coffee.
Please do order something hard
Otherwise she can't shine with her latté art.
She's a thrill seeker all the way, always down for a road trip,
Teeg's killer playlist on play.
Occasionally she likes to dance, those college kids don't
stand a chance.
Yeah when she moves on her own,
The passion, the energy, their minds are blown.
A cool girl all around,
I like the way you are, so honest and profound.

Language of Emotions (Red)

Rage, violence and pain
Arguing and sinful comments
Regret, scars and tears
Twisted sex, lust and dominance
Pulling away and getting closer
A language of bodies filled with remorse.

Seasonal Love

As new buds sprout, new beginnings find their way.
I see a summer dress, crimson red hair, freckles and a tender
smile.
You dance around the flying blossom with a flower in your
hair.
You let the world and all its judgement be as it may and
twirl like you don't care.
Moving around feeling the freshly cut grass beneath your
feet,
Lying down, looking at the sun enjoying its heat.
Closing your eyes, taking it all in
A new season has arrived,
leaving you with a cheeky, little grin.

Jumpy the Goldfish

Once upon a time there was a goldfish named Jumpy.
This was no ordinary goldfish for he was eager to see the
world.
Whenever his owner wasn't home, he swam to the surface of
his bowl, looking out on the living room, wondering what
was beyond.
After much training and preparation he swiftly swam to the
surface once again,
And with every fiber in his body he jumped.
Flying high through the air, for a brief moment, he could
now see through the window of the living room.
He saw the streets of the town, the city lights and a church.
He had heard its bell going off many times but had never
seen how majestic this piece of architecture was.
In this moment of discovery he snapped out of his bubble
and realized he was now a fish on dry land.
Gasping for air, flipping his fins, he soaked up the dust of
the Parisian carpet he was lying on; coloring him grey.
When he thought all was over, his life flashing before his
eyes, his owner came home and saw what had happened.
Just in time, she put him back in his bowl and miraculously
jumpy came back to life.
Now that he had seen what was out there, regardless of the
danger, Jumpy from now on jumped out of his bowl every
day. He was a goldfish with a dream to see the world and he
had pursued his dream for a good 8 years until he passed
away. Rest in peace, Jumpy.

The Train Ride

The door closes
I take my seat
Even if you tried, you couldn't ignore the smell of Thai food
floating around the wagon.
At quite a few spots in the train there's signs saying: "NO
FOOD ALLOWED."
Of course, it's naïve to think people actually find them
relevant.
Normally, the smell would bother me, but not this time.
Across from me, a few benches further, *you* were seated. You
wore a beige crop top and a leather jacket.
Your earrings were music notes and you had your hair in a
messy bun.
You fished a make-up mirror out of your little bag, checking
up on the situation that was your face. The funny bit was
that you were wearing a face mask like everyone else in the
train,
leaving only your eyes on display.
Of course this limitation didn't influence your scream to
express yourself,
as you applied some eye shadow and mascara on your face.
To be fair, you knew what you were doing.
Having a twin sister learns you many things, one is, make
up is an art form.
Her eye for detail was amazing.
She made it so, that her blue eyes looked like a stormy sea,
fierce and intimidating.
I wanted to go up to her and say some cheesy pick up line,
but something told me that I shouldn't.

Before I knew it, I was lost at sea in her eyes, I felt like we were already telling each other stories, getting to know one another.
Every minute this went on longer I felt like you were starting to undress me with your eyes and then...

DING DONG: "NEXT STATION MEIERSPLEIN"

She stood up and left.

The Life of a Tennis Ball

Bounce, bounce, bounce,
Aww, my head hurts.
Bounce, bounce, bounce,
On the field and in their skirts
Bounce, bounce, bounce,
Sometimes filled with rage
Bounce, bounce, bounce,
On the court or on their face
Bounce, bounce, bounce,
Flying through the sky
Bounce, bounce, bounce,
Are we done, no it's a tie (break)

My Mess, a.k.a. My Room

Wrinkled clothes
Dusty desk
Please do enter, this is no test
You might find this dirty
You might find this dumb
But this is the chaos in which I belong
My bookcase is filled with literature all around,
and every so often you'll hear a music sound.
Where you might need a map, or some direction,
I know the exact location of my collection.
The order I have speaks volumes to me,
for this is my own little catastrophe.

Rain's Coming

Clouds start to hug
Trees start to wave
Swallows fly by low
and slowly but steadily, ripples start to form in the water,
leaving pulsing circles
The wind, now really picks up
And those tender tears have now transitioned into weeping
rain showers

and well, I am wet.

EMILY SALT

Emily Salt returned to writing poetry after years immersed in building a family, growing her career in the social sciences, as well as heavy involvement in developing a roller derby league. In March 2019, Emily joined the Instagram poetry community using a pseudonym—as some poets do—to enable uninhibited creative expression.

Known for her quirky and "salty" tone, Emily pushes the reader to dive into real life topics about mental health, relationships, social phenomena and stigma. Don't let this Canadian poet's humble demeanour fool you, Emily is ambitious—although less urgently as she grows wiser.

Above all, Emily values authentic writing and collaborating with artists who share her passion for having fun with words.

With sights set on publishing Emily's debut poetry book soon, you will find her single poem publications in *MIND: A Poetry Anthology Exploring Mental Health* and CovidChronicles.com.

Visit emilysaltpoetry.com or @emilysaltpoetry on Instagram and Facebook to explore more of her works.

Curse of the #Instapoet

Are mainstream poetry algorithms ready to accept
Instagram poets as legitament?
/probably not yet because there I go with typo/
Listen, I'm not going take up arms about the 'insta-curse'
but join me - let's at least take up pens.
Be [a] writer
Be [an] author
Be [the] voice
/notice I didn't say 'be best'/
Be part of the independents' poetry revolution
Write
Share
Any way
Any where
Why fight this bias!
Focus on raising your authentic voice
Embrace being an illegitimate #instapoet
And then reclaim this space
To just be
A writer

At the Core of a Poet

suspended between two points
I sway welcoming fluffy inspirations
cloudy but only partially
taking shapes of Vikings on surfboards
or little feet running down the street
conjured dreams and memories
some too sore if pulled from my core
full extraction would be fatal but go ahead
core me to make some sweet delicious sighs
bite by bite savour these words I bare
with only one request
spare my unsavoury bits from being thrown out
and toss these bitter seeds to the earth
before left forgotten when bellies are full
and my allure has gone with your appetite
wherever I land, I will grow
out of our filthy foundations
renewed from manure
writing verse about versus
and rhymes to reflect on the times
fruits of a poet's emotional labour
yield hope, truth, and power
especially when sown

just write

The Nots

Days like these are more than not
Thinking curves around the clock
Starts out straight, and then it's not
Up and down, and into knots
Stomach turning, calm cannot
Convinced, that's it! Flu I got
Symptoms check, is that a cough?
Maybe, yes? I'm feeling hot
Keep your space - could be caught
But viruses are not from thoughts

Missed the boat, or just forgot
To keep things straight - notes I jot
Lost my notes, it's all for nought
Questions out, she's lost the plot?
Yeah, I'm stressed! You're in earshot
Time to check for answers sought
Did I check my blindest spot?
All I found was a mugshot
Of how I was before onslaught of all the nots
Train of thoughts

Let it Roll

It's the bravest of moments when I start my first task. The next bravest is the following moment when I continue that same task. And then again after I finish that task and I start my second task.

/I think you get it now/

Sometimes seemingly little successes are big ones! Be proud of the littlest ones and let the momentum roll. Eventually these little successes grow up to be big kick-ass successes - just like you.

Release the Elephants

These elephants don't despair
No-one's bothering to acknowledge them anyway
Big or tiny
These grey marvels are getting comfy
There's one on the couch
Over there and under here...
Where? /Under here! /
Under where? /You said, Underwear! /
There's one in my mouth
Ready to jump out
And when it lands the impact could be minimal
Or perhaps somewhat abysmal
Usually makes someone uncomfortable
And that's the reason most stay hidden
Elephants are heavy
Even when on their tip toes
Dancing to your favourite kid's show
Perhaps you already know the ending to this poem

Ready to finish the last line for me?
Give it a try, just think...

Elephants belong wild, not under your kitchen ___.

Sigh Master

These
These feelings
These feelings suffocate
These feelings suffocate thoughts
These feelings suffocate thoughts relentlessly
These feelings suffocate
These thoughts
These
These thoughts embrace
These thoughts embrace acceptance
These thoughts embrace acceptance tentatively
These thoughts embrace
These feelings

Thoughts and feelings at odds
Teetering the balance of wellness to illness
Illness to wellness; wellness to illness...
Pause. Breathe.
Sit down - so as not to fall
Pause. Breathe.
Take a stand - make it tall
Up and down; down and up
Work it out between each sigh
Just like a mindful little Sigh Master

Grasping Memories

Care-free and sweet
Pigtails, bare feet
Unaware of tragedy she will meet
Running in tall grass and Queen Anne's lace
Punctuated with dandelion puffs and daisies
She'll play with no set beginning or ending
Today, it will be house under the willow tree
Entering the front door through curtained branches
That transform into swaying strips of wallpaper
Sometimes she pretends they are moustaches
Acting out the roles of those she looks up to
Being mommy and sister, then teacher
Braiding crowns with jewels made of thistles
Preparing rock stews with wiggly caterpillar pickles
Naptimes are as short as saying they happened
And the play continues…

When the sun dips lower
The shade gets cooler
Long branches slap at her chilly cheeks
Dinnertime must be near
She'll stretch each minute until her daddy carries her in over
his shoulder
And here he is…

Away they go
Her small hands grasp a branch

Each leaf pops off as she gets carried away
Tossing willow leaf bliss in the air
Her heart is bursting to the tippy top
With a kiss, he sets her down inside the door

"Time to eat", he says
But she is not hungry
Not even for ice cream with berries
Too full grasping at these memories
Before she forever lost her dear sweet daddy

I Know How

I know how you can stop being anxious.

      Quit worrying and just be where you are.

But we know that you'll never be satisfied staying anywhere and soon you'll get bored.

I know how you can avoid getting bored.

      Stop being where you are.

Sinking All In

I'm leading with my toes
As I head towards the uncertain
Little dip
Check it quick
Seems ok enough
Maybe even good enough
For standing in
Submerged up to my ankles
/also called ankle-deep/
Long enough to test the waters
For sinking in
No need for waders
Best way to be in
Is all in
Then I can
Feel the currents
Drifting through the sediment
Call me Twinkle Toes when I'm
Getting to the bottom of it
On my pointed tipsy toes
Quite different than
Flat-footed stomps of the masses
Especially when too shallow
They make muddy rivers impassable
Once I'm deeper in
I find my place here
Keeping akin

To the mighty and free
Seeking to be non-tidally pristine
Yet the storms will come again
Untamed
I stand firm
Until the fury ripples away
Returning when?
This is hard to know
Nevertheless
Breaks are welcome
I bathe in the freshwater
When I can enjoy the fruits of
Dipping my toes
Wading up to my nose
Wiggly little piggies
Beautifully caught up in the
Stream of it all

Headliner Amour

Listen
Can you hear it?
Hearts beating one octave higher
Then lower
Arpeggios three
Melodically drumming
Off-beats
Then on-beats
New loves match tempo

No one's asleep
Counting bars better than counting sheep

1,   2,   3,   4

Snare drum sweep

Can't tell whose love sings more
On this lullaby tour

From the Inside

I'm changing inside
I'm not the same
More or less sane
More than less I'm feeling the rain
Nothing is mundane
Threads of existence swirl
Changing my fabric
World full of habits
Rearranged or dropped
Tears dried up
All mopped
History's lessons rewatched
Rethought
Restocked
Next level unlocked
Bullshit uncocked
Gratitude pouring out my seams
From the inside

Nowhere Close to Getting It

Introducing my cheeks
As eaves dripping fearsome frustration
Rolling into pools of collared ravines where I
Bathe in somber sobriety
Reflecting on the whether forecast
More rain projected
Filling flooded lands
Broke the damn

Meet my ribs
As the instrument rising and falling
Playing monotonous tunes often mistaken for
Accordion blues
Steadily slow vibrations taking in all and
Letting out little more than a sigh
Next phrasing the same
Bars upon bars
Scores of a bilateral caged heart

Homage to my belly
As the reservoir of gutted dreams that
Digest then purge making room for products of a
Sustenance seeking appetite often left wanting more
Glutton, I say
Be grateful for crumbs some days
Swollen cavity, yet so empty

Stand at attention from kneeling knees
As a symbol of solidarity
Forced upon us by starch-collared monsters
Progressive troubles from
Decades unwilling to budge without more and more
Coffin nudges tallied higher
Yet still, we are on our knees
Watching
Silent
Filling communities with grief
Writing with tormented tones and cries for change

And still... nowhere close to getting it

NATHANIEL CHIN

London-based Nathaniel Chin (@natty.chin) is a self-described wanderer, dreamer, divorcee, former Evangelical, and current idealist. He writes to share his experiences and existential thoughts; rational, metaphysical, and anything in between.

He's been writing for three years and builds his works upon a foundation of religious learnings and challenges, his attempt to interweave this with his purpose for living, his struggles, opinions, virtues, and cravings. Often these works pose more questions than answers. But, what's the point of living if you have nothing to learn anyway?

"My hope is that my works, or should I say our works, as a compartment of our collective being helps each one of us on our journeys, provokes thought, lightens burdens, and opens doors to our authentic selves."

Power to the People

There's no virtue in virtue signaling,
Just unreasonable doubt.
There's no point in empty gestures,
When there's looting and there's riots.
Egocentric celebrities and SJWs picking fights,
And battles filled with hashtags,
Politicians and alt-rights.
With a trickle of fickle words,
That go viral for some 'Likes'.
I don't care about your white guilt,
Even less for being 'woke',
When we're seen as parodies,
And entertainment for the masses.
From MLK to BLM,
This has been our destination.
Giving voices to our people,
With no privilege, and with no name.
Educating and enlightening,
Those who are miseducated.
To remove the spell of victimhood,
That segregates our races.

Breathless

Today I was unwilling to take a stand or bend a knee.

Reluctant to lend a hand, unable to turn the other cheek.

Complicit in your eugenics by virtue of my acquiescence.

But in truth, I wished to glorify the virtues that evolved from
my genetics.

But then the product of my expression was placed in chains.

And then the emanations of my convictions were exposed.

Lacerated, and emasculated with metaphysical scars.

Neck pressed,

Breathless beneath the tread of your boot,

And the weight of your sins.

You necessitated the defecation of my spiritual essence.

Engrained within my vessel on this physical plane.

Yet, in my precognition is the truth of your obsession.

Infatuated with my presence, enchanted by my gaze.

As you acknowledge the divinity of my 'so called' flaws.

Intersectionality

You have a disdain for my complexion,
Except, let me dispel such a generalisation,
For I am adored by some but abhorred by others.
The complexities of ethnicities vying for power,
Fighting for a plate and a seat at the table of those who sit in
shadows.
Or should I say some table scraps and a foot stool?
Serving microaggressions like Scooby Snacks.
But, if the enemy of my enemy be my friend,
Then why are we hated by all nations?
Not that I believe the hype, but I'd rather have a heated
debate,
With my 'others' from another mother.
And yet should I feel guilty for fraternising with the so-
called enemy?
I'm not afraid to be black and to love another colour.
Yet you're not willing to set your own hatred aside on both
sides.
An agent of miscegenation, multiculturalism, and
affirmative action.
Pro-black and pro-wack.
But for the sake of my own peace of mind,
Let's define those blurry lines.
Am I a product of my melanin, my gender, or my social
class?
Moreover, what is the measure of my manhood and my
demographic?
Except excuse me for my lack of pronouns and definitions.
Interracial, intersexual and gender fluid,
Beyond the flesh, and blood and marrow.
But if I were to be defined by a word,

I'd be a metaphor,
The archetype of meaning and divine inspiration.
A Neoplatonic spark,
Cast in brown skin.
Born within the caste
Of the working-class hero.

Quarantine Daydreams

Folding clothes and washing dishes,

But my wishes extend beyond these chores.

And my vices extend beyond these walls,

But her walls are far away.

Feelings that lie beyond all reason,

That require some contemplation,

But I digress as I complain in isolation.

In seven chambers of dissension,

Filled with thoughts of First World Problems.

Fluctuations of frustrations,

Notions echo and evolve.

Cloaked around hallucinations,

Sparking forms and revelations,

In the seven other kingdoms of creation.

Conjoined with other machinations of the mind.

Blind Faith

I think that I believe in what I see,
Even though I cannot trust my own sight.
Merely a grandiose mirage, and barrage of colours,
Backhanded by the phantoms in the white of my lies.
By the sight of my reflection and the beam within my eye.
A rose tinted, and wooden, and gross observation.
Masked by dark figures and shades of allegory.
Allegedly, figuratively.
Speaking of which,
Is it my true intention to see my own true intentions?
Or do I desire to embrace my own Maya?
A cuckhold to her wiles and flirtations,
And seductive soliloquies.

To Live Another Time

Thoughts cast back upon epochs and ages,
Bearing witness to my own gestation.
Those were the days when I wished to ask, "Why"?
Yet lacked the words to speak, and the skills to write.
A bastion of knowledge in the mind of an infant,
Lifetimes' lived and condensed within the form of a babe.
Fulfilling prophecies, breaking promises, and crushing your
dreams.
Dreams cast aside mountains as dry bones.
Speaking life into corpses, whilst digging their graves.
As the hero and villain of my own making.
Shedding light and not blood to the delight of many,
At least on this occasion.
Descending through various phases of substance and matter.
Shortlisted from time and space,
To purposely purchase the souls that I've murdered,
And vanquish their demons in vain.
With visions and dreams of my God given purpose,
Yet lacking the right to perceive.
Oh, to be an immortal convicted by dead men,
Redeeming my conscience forever!

Thyme

I tend to go about my daily life within reason, but without rhyme. A perpetual, insulated, pseudo-singularity. Bland, short of sight and narrow of mind.

But from time-to-time I forget that the rhythm of thyme does not gyrate with the movers and shakers, nor step to the beat of the many moons, feasts, and stars, nor observance the high and most holy places. For thyme is not sprinkled to the letter of the law and its diverse doctrines and recipes, but scattered with liberty, abundant in levity and bereft of mortal brevity.

This is the great taste of life, the never-ending marinade. It was written that eye has not seen, nor ear heard. But I have indeed tasted, and it is good. Indeed, we have all tasted, and now savour that inner saviour.

Anomalous Me

Am I the anomaly?
Swimming and flip-flapping within the bowls of this
primordial soup.
Moreover, swarmed over by the broth and the froth as I
slosh in indignation.
Anonymous to the anatomy and the strategy of the status
quo.
Stratified and radicalised into a living, breathing non-
sequitur,
An absurdity, nay an oddity!
As I stood upon the precipice of perilous thoughts and
flights of fancy,
I fancied my chances and took a stand
Against the tide of this imporous and predestined ooze.
Thick with oodles of murmurs, and memoirs, and legends.
That speak of my beginnings, my belongings, and that
which I would come to be.
But I say, by whose will dictate my becoming?
For the hearsay of the sages is naught but for stuffing.
And the provisions of our living are only fit for the rabid.
And my sovereignty is defined by your heresy.
As a lover of my own inner choices.
And a voyeur to your own outer vices.
My very own light and constellation, a collection of
exceptions, and complex connotations.
Surrounded, and enshrouded by expanses of dark and grey
matter.
As a matter of fact, it was the 'fact' of your matter.
That gave voice to the matters of my heart.

Who Am I?

I came in peace.

My vessel has traversed many great ravines, realms, and perils. Where darkness obscures the sight, and a great chill infects the bones. Learning but never knowing, drinking but ever thirsty.

A fleeting high, and then starvation, followed by seductive whispers, whimpers and tremors that bring castration, and a faint hope that brings damnation. I become lost, dissected, dismembered and inhuman.

Weary of the daily drudgery, trudging back and forth in the rot of entropy. And so, stuck in this rut I wonder of distant realms, planes, and lucid dreams. Face-to-face, with who I was, who I am and who I yet hope to be.

It was written that foxes have holes, and the birds have nests, and that I have no place to rest my head, but my true home rests within the heart of infinity. Not in the grave, nor the cross, nor the infernal fires of the astral hells, nor the myriad matrices and fabrications of the gurus, godmen, and Galactic Federations.

Who am I to challenge the will of those who have bound sweet Pleiades? And loosed the bands of Orion?

Who am I?

The Musings of a Nihilist

A cacophony of melodies and remedies.
Concocted and distilled into various bottles, and potions, and lotions.
Taking two of these, and one of those...once, and twice a day.
They call it therapeutic, but I call it corrective, coercive, and divisive.
Estranged from the pains and the strains of a weird and wonderful tonic.
The makings of an emotional masochist, flinching and wincing from life's many lashes and gashes.
That fuels and excites my resolve and absolves me of all my pity.
That pities both the fool and the pious, who make a living off a pittance.
Is this what it means to exist?
To live and let love in silence and loathing?
Mumbling and miming to endless homilies and harmonies?
A big wet dream in a meme, with no climax?
I guess that your guess, is as good as mine.

No-Ledge

I've seen those, who seem to know something.
They parade the streets with stern grins and steely smiles,
rich in pearly whites and flashy rags. Their eloquence is
preceded by the pretence of unassuming 'ums' and 'ahs'.
Going through the motions of choruses and versus,
rehearsed in attack and decay.
They preach with all their twisted and vaunted vanity.
Rubbing the hard-grey bristles, and razor-sharp bumps that
line their swelling faces; inflamed by harsh notes and the
taste of moonshine in the light of day. Huffing and puffing,
against the gnawing white noise of the urban sprawl.
Wrapping verbs and hooks around flying fists to do battle
and brattle, with all who live and move and have their own
being.
And it seems to me, that they know nothing at all.

The Box Delusion

I tried to fit into Pandora's Box, labelled with a brand, and
some stickers. Stacked in lines of rows and aisles.
Packaged to protect the heart and suppress the mind,
confined to the archives of a time and times past tense.
Beneath the corrugated flaps, the bubble wrap, and the
scotch tape there was fragile, colourless glass, or so I'd been
told.
As I perched on my shelf I was impelled, impaled by the
protrusions of the splinters' taunts and doubts; and my
contents felt cold, hard and shallow.
I no longer wished to conform to the length, width, and
height of my container.
But I was hollow in my thoughts, and filled myself with
pretty trinkets, gems and shiny things that rust and break.
They were put on sale; idolised, placed on pedal stools and
praised in high places.
And I was torn apart from the inside-out, turned-out, naked,
and gutted for my possessions.
My fate was unfolding.
To be buried in a scrap yard grave, recycled into pulp.
Or fitted and stitched together like some carboard cut-out.
A freak of glue and paper, and of nature.
In my next reincarnation.

The Hook Up

You sent me a voice note.
I could hear the sharp chords in your voice.
A series of bittersweet melodies, that make mention of a
simpler season.
A melancholy transition,
Fractured syllables,
Imperfect prose and pronunciation.
Followed by the swelling and groaning of unkind and
colourful verbs.
Accosted by a palette of cruel expletives chased with honey.
I'm turned on, unaccustomed to your curses.
But crushed by your disdain for my feelings.
A glutton for punishment I suppose,
An ejaculation of untamed slurs.
Unchained, off the hook, and off the tip of the tongue.
But whilst I appreciate your oral stimulation,
My soul aches and my heart quakes for a purer kind of
connection.
A 'Down to Earth', 'Shaking my Foundations' kind of love.
Grown from healthy soils and foundations,
And not just the soiling of my pants.

Poetic Apologetics

I was told to dispose of my verses.
Expected to down tools in the face of conformity.
But homogeny has never been in my vocabulary.
Given the chance you'd have me acting the fool and the minstrel.
Tap dancing, and shuckin' and jivin'
But what am supposed to do?
Should I repress this rising fire, or be consumed by it?
As if I've emerged from Plato's cave unscathed,
Only to turn back and reattach my chains.
Bound by clichés and Great Heresies,
A farcical of logical fallacies eloquently posed and repurposed.
But that is not my true purpose.
For I've been chosen to sire a babe and some lyrics in the midst of the desert.
That is destined to become a voice that cries in the wilderness.
 For out of the mouths of babes have we perfected our praise.
That I proclaim is the way, and the truth and the light.
That does away with Fight or Flight,
Replaced with Flights of Fancy.

Anthony James Rivera

Young Latin man
Puerto Rican blood
Electrician
Born in June
Ruled by the moon
But I'm also handy with some tools

Yes, I'm from Connecticut
Waterbury to be exact
Travel the east coast for work
So catch me when I get back

26 years this year
Pink glasses and long hair
Man of my word
And I like to use my words

So this was just a glimpse
I'm convinced on your interest
Read along and get pulled in
I hope my words can make you grin

-Anthony James Rivera
@_antrivera

123

Friends

Good friends did good riddance once I had them for the
night
But once I had them once or twice
It went left, never right
Now I'm looking for a friend
But there isn't one in sight

Baking Bread

Tried to take my bread and butter
Just so they could have some cake
Only took the tools eat
'Cause I still know how to bake
The set back is the yeast
Give it time, my numbers rise
You don't wanna see a feast
I suggest you close your eyes
While I'm sitting at the table
Trying to keep the balance stable
With all this cake
It seems I got the syrup maple
Won't catch me separating
Keep it together like a staple
Thru the night I'll keep a shine
Just like the sun brings day glow

Complimentary Being

For every one man on this earth
There are three women in the same space
Now that makes sense since women are a personification of
water and water covers 3/4s of the earth
Women being wild, free, loving, life bringing
Are all characteristics of water
Water is free and will do what it pleases as we've seen in the
shapes of tsunamis and the ocean
Water will crash and wash away anything that comes
between its path
It will shape the earth and create rivers as well as drown
volcanos and valleys
Yet man, which cannot be the land, nor the beast cultivates
the earth to spread his seed
He moves mountains and trowels trenches to give life
direction
The water reflecting now moves toward the seeding section
where the man can plant
Now they become a team
Man domesticates the land to create resources to give the
water direction to create civilization.
Without water, man has no life.
So man must learn not to control woman
For they can never be controlled
The ocean can sink the unsinkable
Water smothers flames and causes earth to slide
He must learn to maneuver through her
Weathering her waves
Knowing there will be a brighter day
He must not divert her
For her force drives her current and keeps her going

Rather clear and cultivate the route for her to flow freely
To be open and expressive at her loudest roar
And the calmest stream
And that is complimentary being

Discipline

Discipline is the difference
From moving militant
And detriment
Move incorrect &
It'll rob you of your innocence
But in a sense
It just makes sense
For you
to stick to your guns
Try to make amends
And change the plan
And then you're done
I bet that if you kept your step
You'd never get off track
It takes some stress just give your best
It'll always pay you back

Learning to Detach

Learning to detach
Letting go to bring me back
I was drowning in my brain
Pain of falling off the raft

Swam down, unplugged the drain
Saw the product of my pain
Grey matter turned to waste
As I fill up my ash trays

Days are quick to pass
While they spin, I get the bag
I got a God-given gift
I just use it to give back

Giving back to make me grin
Healing homes from within
Starts a spark in my heart
I do my part, the people win

Loose Change

Making sense of things
is too high a price to pay
'Cause nowadays
Everybody's only filled with change
They give their two cents
When your bills already paid
Funny thing is
Most of them pay theirs late
If I charged for common sense
Some would say it's too great
Still give their hand out
With a hand full of change
If you turn them away
Things surely start to change
Like a quarter on the loose
It's all rolling down the drain

Shedding Light

And they see how bright you shine
Fiends will try to snuff you out
'Cause your candle's lighting up some minds
Information is the dime
that nobody seems to drop
Like you gotta find it on your own
'Cause it'll turn your bros to opps
Time to open up shop
'Cause I got some things to build
These institutions are a shill
Front like they're tryna help you heal
I feel I gotta do my part
Give a spark, change a life
Open hearts, build an ark
So those that ARE the change will ride

Voices of the Unheard

Riots filled with violence
Since they haven't listened to words
They couldn't take the knee from #7
So why did he press his knee for 9
A blatant slap in the face
Would have you going out your mind
Going on for years since this isn't the first time
If you know you have a voice
It's only right to speak your mind
Signs all around screaming messages of truth
Every black life should matter in a nation built off you

Take a Stand

Burdens you don't ask seem to fall on top of yours
If you try to stack more
End up fallin' thru the floor
Falling down breeds a new chance to take a stand
When the burdens not your own
Holding on will hurt your hand
When you stand alone
No one else can take your stance
The shoes might fit
But only you can wear the pants

Starstruck

We spend our life looking up tryna reach the stars
Becoming one seems to fill obsession in our hearts
Years flow by so the reach starts getting far
Age sets in, wrinkles get confused with scars
Still not alone, the others slash across your mind
You run around in circles while you're running out of time
 just to make the next move while you try to make a dime.
Once the penny's spent & gave your last two cents,
 still coming up short when you try to make some sense.
Annihilate your fears, release all your stress
If you have to shed some tears, it'll sew up all your chest.
Lay you down to rest even though you left a scar
You finally got your wish, now we wish upon a star

Free Spirit

Smoke swirls with the wind
As it hits her bare skin
Gazing out
As she thinks about
Her night full of sin
Ashes dance from her grin
To her it's a win
She won't be contained
Refuse to refrain
Her spirit is free
Since it's free from within

Smooth Stone

Stone turns smooth from the way water moves
Across its surface to make it perfect
It's ironic that it soothes
Wear away the imperfections
To the edges with persistence
It'll make a certain texture with reflections in its image
In addition to omittance it provides a chance to change
If water always finds its level think like water's on the brain
Even when you take a shower water washes all the pain
When you wanna take a trip, pick your ship
And drift away
If you been living in the rain, you don't have to feel
estranged
It doesn't only rain in April and not every flower blooms in
May
It's crazy 'cause when you drown
The water causes pain and strife
But when you're down and in a drought
You pray for rain
'Cause it brings life

Cody James

I have always sought the chaos of life and darkest of alleys way to frolic, dance and skip down with no remorse of the aftermath or whom I hurt in the process; believing I was a cat with nine lives to do as I please. Here I sit, typing away with a crib to my back and a rocking horse to my left currently on my thirteenth life. My last one and the very best by far. My name is Cody James; I am currently 33 years of age. I am hopelessly bound to a woman who I have been with for close to a decade, and a father of one to my daughter Wilde Ann. To put into perspective of my love for literature I have named my little one after Oscar Wilde, whom I put as number one on my list of influences.

Writing, rhythm, verse and song have always called to me. Nothing has made me feel more worthwhile than writing a beautiful line or describing what it is to smash a glass against the wall in the most unique and awkward way without having to physically follow through with the act. Words possess power. Words can touch the soul. Words can warm the heart. Words can cut to the bone.

These are my words. Thank you for reading.

Beauty Squandered

Frantic, manic, friendly fiend

Where did you come from?

A conscious thought

Brief may it be

Of right or wrong

What's wrong?

The ideals: that have been without permission might I add
thrust upon my soul?!

A shotty disposition of what I should or should not do

No real concrete sentence.

I painfully ponder the level perfect horizon

The earth may be flat after all

Oh I am full of fucking shit

We want the world and we want it!

Not your perfect, pretty purple plastic estates

Conveyor belt children

Collapsed veins

I long for my own mound of dirt

My own family

Put myself on a cross for you

And I will mind you...trust these words

Freely flowing furious lines

Lovely literature

What does my mind consist of?

What does my heart yearn for?

What does my soul scream for?

Painfully obviously I humbly admit

I want to be ready when I take that roundabout

Full circle

And ironic, redundant beautiful end

Let's go smoke some crack

Beauty squandered.

Cell Ceiling Blues

I'm here to deep clean

Spring clean

My cell ceiling blues

Scrub the remnants and tenements of past souls whom knew just what to do

Commandments

Silly little clown shoes

I know you'd like to see me swing in my cell awhile

Piles and miles

I've crawled over like a baby searching for the tit

Coffee is amazing

My day is just learning to walk, please allow time

I've walked miles

Found silver hiding in the ashes of yesterday

We smile though a plastic poorly made mask

I walk with my hellhound

Choke chain

Short leash

Snuffed myself an angel

Cut her deep

Cut her through the wings

Freeing myself

Free

I am free

Still would like a glass or four of whiskey

Aged older than me

Pour me

poor me

Madness.

Tin Foil Lullabies

He walks through a door to find ravishment

Dumbfounded and bewildered

Moreover, TOO bewitching to refrain

One man says Venus

The other Madonna

And I say you…

Scared and lost my girl?

Me too.

Hop along. Hideaway. Run.

Dream a little dream

Just a little

Can't hurt

Just a little

Good to feel

Just a little

A cynic. Life.

Stale mate

Checkmate

Foolish thoughts

Wicked games

Gone fishin'

Just a little

Fly. Fall. Free.

Seedy, mom's home cookin' back alleyways

Sappy stories

Philosophical, cave riddled allegories

Nice cave and Pluto drinking whiskey

Socrates with green eyes

Can we debate the holy trinity?

Sad, redundant misled children

Nothing more to say

We didn't tentatively listen

Gain a little perspective

Close your eyes. Shut down.

Smile

Just a little

Laugh

Just a little

Love my girl.

Bye. Hello. What?

30 years of countin' cards

What comes after the ace of spades?

Structured stanza

Lyrical, rhythmic thought out lines

If I whisper pretty nothings can your panties be mine?

Pour myself into oblivion

Poor me

Fade away

Out.

Love you sons a bitches

Bye.

Hello.

Bellow obscenities

Filthy little liars.

Just a little

Dirty, pretty things

My lovelies

Dark as man's mind

Sweet as sin

Ever let the devil in?

Humbled opinions that can be tested

Opium in a pipe is a soul well rested

Fun little trips to the eccentric

Lips of the magnificent

Hips of the hypnotic

Wills that can be tested

By words

Syllabled and miracles

Takes ONE ear

Fix them. I'll be okay.

Post me up and whip me

Grand moments of delicacy

It's all bullshit

Lies and jargon

Sweet, roll on the floor tooth rotting duplicity

Charles Lutwidge Dodgson was brutally brilliant

Even though this poem is a load of jabberwocky.

Hyde Away

Disappointment

Regret of the most violent of nature

Embarrassment and sorrow for you my friend

This hand will no longer be one I shall ever lend

A leech.

A tapeworm.

Parasite.

Ones who's destined to lose

Boy you ain't nothing but a piece of dog shit stuck to the bottom of clown shoes.

Nothing but a hangman's noose

Side by side

I was beggin' to lose

Like a man I can admit the web you wove

I was stuck

I was stuck

They say the grass is always greener.

And now I am free

I thank you for the lessons you so selfishly taught me

And now my soul feels clean

And now my soul feels clean

How I forgot what it is to soundly sleep

I pray the only time we ever meet

Will be in my dreams

For I still have nightmares Mr. Hyde

For I still have nightmares.

Madhouse Sessions

Time tactfully ticks whereas my shadow wanes willfully

Long to wax

The boy in the mirror is gone today

The man in the mirror is here to stay

Sunken hollow eyes.

Gleefully gaunt.

Dark familiar circles.

Nothing is random.

To be sober, I once hear a mad man eloquently rapping,

"Is like walking around with no skin and the wind is blowing"

No setting sail today I must say

No tacky named boat either

Nothing but a cracked chimney

A crooked picture frame

Slouched, sad faced caricatures wallow through a dim, musky pee riddled hallway

Dragging the yellow soles of their feet

Defeated desperation

Boredom.

Ennui.

I wish my crayon had an eraser.

16 Gallons of Gasoline

You weigh as much as 16 gallons of gasoline

No matter the quality of grade

I've found out many of times

Your bout as combustible

My horse who cannot be tamed

You plucked my name from the dead letter file

Forgotten

No return address

Opened my envelope and recite my words

Sipping poison from a chardonnay glass

Crack open the whiskey and light us a square

Roulette with gas a flame

No longer forgotten

Love letters lost and rotten

My horse who cannot be tamed.

Chattanooga

I fail to write the words that I long for you to read

I fail to hold you when you are scared

So, you sleep sweet

Whiskey

My Achilles

Chains that stretch far

From Portland to Tennessee

I fail to love you right

Though I love you in my way

Wars made in the name of God

God

Can we please start subscribing to God being a female?

I fail though

I fail

I fail

I failed.

Here with Me

you are the light that no man deserves

although you are here

I've seen colors burst from your smile that have healed
centuries old wounds in the catacombs of my soul

I never deserved love

I never deserved love like this

although you are here

universe growing

galaxies glowing

deep in your eyes I finally see

sirens songs now faint and far

hellhounds caged lock and bar

I will forever strive to give you the best of me

you are the verse I can never write

although you are here

you are the song I could never play

although you are here

my protector, my shield

my daughter, my queen

miracles never happen

although you are here

you are here

here

here with me.

DAVIAN WILLIAMS

Davian Williams, born in Somerville, New Jersey, is an aspiring artist who indulges in storytelling with poetry at his forefront. Also influenced by music, photography, and film, Williams provides strong imagery while questioning concrete ideals to create an authentic and personal experience for the audience to enjoy. Stay tuned for his upcoming first publication, *Live From The Limbic System*.

Instagram - @willz_the.cameraman
Facebook – Davian Williams

Location Unknown

In between the back of your head

And right under your nose,

There's a place that we know

Without a name.

That special place where you can't tell

If the lucid dream has started

Or consciousness has ended.

Like when you squint your eyes

And the colors stretch for miles.

Or like you finally close them

And see more than just the darkness.

Imagination's little loopwormhole

Into reality's open world.

Life's dime-sized doggydoor

Into the realm of thought.

You'll know you're there

If it looks like a dreamer's trip, but

Feels like a tripper's dream.

Crash & Burn

Out of focus and energetic,

Like a sugar rush high,

Uplifting and euphoric, but

Only for a moment.

Such an attachment can be so strong that

I'll stay strapped in

Even for the crash.

The pain tends to linger

Even after the scars heal,

The bruises fade,

And the stomach aches subsides,

Making it that much harder

To acquit it from my memory.

Bet It All on Hearts

Money speaks loudly in a casino,

But could never outstand

The worth of a man's words.

The game of love is

A gamble with your emotions.

When it's time to pay up,

The fee hurts more than your wallet.

The damage done to your heart,

Irreversible,

All for a price not worth a penny.

Breaking the Laws of Attraction

Day after day,

My mind spends its time

Binge watching the thought of you.

Countless episodes,

Like the one when your smile

Broke my heart.

Or the one when you left me

Lost in your eyes.

Seasons go by and

The viewers are left to wonder

If I'll ever reach

Enough character development

To become the protagonist

Of my own story.

And the reality is that

I'm more than just the star.

I'm the god damn director

Of this full-length motion picture.

Born to feel passionate,

Born to be passionate,

And my muse was always far beyond

The limits of your lopsided love.

"Lonely Nights" in E Minor

When you tune out of reality,

It gets real quiet.

That other place is

An unlimited void,

Nothing to see,

Unless you're looking for it.

Recently, I stumbled upon a song,

Hiding in between my bones.

A spooky little bass riff

Rocking my spine,

The beat is pulsing

Through all my nerve endings,

And my skin, it sings.

A lively and lonely ballad

About how it craves to be caressed.

And as many times as I've heard it,

It never gets old.

One With Myself

It's better to be in the void.

In between

The all of the universe.

Just outside of will

And beyond fate.

Where the power

Of your own control

Can defeat any and

All of darkness.

For you are

The light that you seek.

And the journey to your answer

May feel like it's never near,

But when you find it,

It'll feel like

It was always a part of you.

Quitting for the Better

My life's epic gradually continues as

The story's protagonist embraces

The next chapter of his journey.

The path to being the best means

You must always be

Better. Every Single Time.

It's important to move forward, but

Never burn your bridges.

It's important to travel light because

Carrying the weight of any burden

Can be the difference between

Climbing to the top

And falling to the bottom.

And if you get the opportunity,

Treat yourself right.

There's no harm in spoiling yourself

In a congratulatory manner.

Just don't let the fumes go to your head.

New Year Like No Other

At eye level,

I look around to see

Faded leaves and frosted trees.

A typical view for a

Cold and snowless winter sunset.

I search in its direction,

But the sun hides behind

All on the horizon line,

Casting a shadow on

Everything in my sight line.

The sun, however, has not set yet.

Perfectly peeking over my head,

I look into the trees and up to the hills.

The background, bathed in oranges

Against a periwinkle sky.

I'd have to say,

Even the most beautiful snowfalls

Couldn't compare to the way that

The heavens just opened up

On the new year.

A Confession

The truth is

I can't not love you.

I really couldn't, even if I tried.

I think it's wrong that

I look for the love we shared in others.

It's not fair to the feelings

I know nothing about.

It's not fair!

We both deserve love,

Just not from each other.

You made it clear that mine

Had no value to you and that yours

Wasn't worth the time we spent.

It's not fair that you're not here,

But your place in my heart

Never seems to leave.

It's wrong because I'd like

To be let someone else make me happy.

I'd like to forget that

You ever happened to me.

I'd really just love to hate you

Because you snipped

The strings to my parachute

And now I'm afraid to free fall.

Writer's Morals

Being away for awhile

Gives you more to write about.

Countless dreams and conversations

To talk about, but

There's a certain bliss that arrives

When you get to interpret

Your own stories.

The feeling of telling the tale

Makes having your own voice

Worth all the while.

So, sometimes,

It's ok to put the pen down.

Sure, we'd love to hear your words, but

We'd much rather hear

What you want to say than

What you want us to hear.

Hitting the Mark

When put to the test,
The probability of success
Can never be calculated.
Because the chances of
Another person surprising you
With literally <u>ANYTHING</u>
Is always one in a million.
But compared to
The world's population,
That's pocket change.
I hate to ramble, but
What I mean is
Fearing the worst
Can't make it better.
And something new
Can be just as frightening,
But at the cost of happiness,
How much are you willing to spend?

The Ever-Lasting Heart-Stopper

A daily dose of dopamine

For the average reader.

The smell of coffee in the air.

The sun stretches out

Over a warm carpet.

The room widens to show

Windows that reach the ceiling

And a grand piano, seated in the center

For the best view.

As I loiter behind the keys,

She asks if I play.

My response isn't yes, but

I do know a song.

I beckon her to sit beside me

And from the first note I play,

The room begins to fill up with

More than just light.

The sounds of curiosity

Radiating throughout the room,

Almost like you can see

Particles of pure imagination

Shimmering in the air.

My heart speaks on the strings of the piano,

Singing the song through my fingers.

It sounds like being above the clouds,

Feels like the back of my head.

A melodic hum that

Rolls its way around the scale.

Some notes are soft and sweet

Like a smooch behind the ear

And some are as bold as

The risk of a first kiss.

But the song is always like a first date;

Memorable, attention-grabbing,

And guaranteed to give anyone's

Butterflies butterflies.

A view of paradise

That defies explanation.

Quadratic Emotions

Intimacy is just a chemical imbalance,

Just like any other math equation.

For example, if we share a thousand smiles,

And laughed the whole night,

And I look into your eyes one more time,

What are the chances

That you'd want to kiss me back?

Hues of Blue

Ocean Spray and Smiles

As the sun lays down to rest.

When the beach and the sky get together,

They love to show off...

Gradients.

The sky was radiant.

Like it was painted by aliens.

I couldn't dare to count the hues.

There was yellow and purple and red and orange

And a billion different blues.

The ocean was like a tide pool.

The darkness turned out the lights

And left the stars to shimmer like some night jewels.

And the sand was pretty nice too.

A fancy drink with some ice cubes

And a little lime.

Smearing the horizon line

In small amounts of time.

I'm in a paradise

And smelling salt in the air.

But I wouldn't know if I was never there.

Jumping Out the Atmosphere

Soaring where the sun can see me,

It feels like I've left

All the heavy lifting

Back on the ground.

There's not a care in the world

That could reel me back into orbit.

I'm just not one to be

Tethered for nothing.

Attraction is stranger than gravity

And can reach across solar systems.

So, if gravity wants to keep me tied to this planet,

Then the earth better tighten its grip.

CARL STRAUT-COLLARD

Carl "Carlito" Gabriel Straut-Collard (c. 1994) is a Brooklyn-native poet, writer, activist, data analyst and Co-Founder of Brooklyn Artist Social, a collective showcase of local visual artists, musicians and performers. He lives and works in the confines of the five boroughs. You can follow him on Instagram @carlgabriel.poetry and expect to see his debut collection *Empire Sunsets* published by Lost Fox Publishing in February 2021.

A Dreamer in New New York

For Allen Ginsberg,
Who Dragged Me From The Sewer
Into the Sunflower

What New Visions I have of you Ginsberg
on this dreamy night when I walk under bluesy east coast
streetlights
searching for the all-elusive Soul Power
that's hiding in the blacked-out shadows
of a broken moon
like a mirage

I ponder at the swooping skyscrapers
with the thought
of how high shall I climb to
fly

You ran with your wailing words until
the pigeons hustled you and left ya broke
right?

My ears are stuffed to the brim with candle wax candy
in this noisy arcade collective of granite
Brick marble glass stones and bones
I only hear the howling glares and moans

Am I also capable of bouncing off bubble-caged walls and
counting
to countless infinities like you must've dreamt
in those hazy hallucinations of Blake and Walt?

I see the neo-millennia eroding at the seams in the wake of
your latest hour
How do I shape my American generation
and those that follow
to be conscious of the fleeting flowers?

Will we always mightily suffer
from the perilous practices of maxed-out greed
and impious power? Racism? Materialism?
Conformity? Alienation?

Starvation of the heart and mind???

I long to grip your fidgety fingers and skip past
the crumbling infrastructure
howling at the fascists
tricking them to glare into the sun's heavy stare

How we'd convene on a perfect park bench to criticize
the soul-doubting senators in this postmodern spiritual
decay
tossing tulips and hum bomb's into the wild winds
naked-minded and free of our credit history

We'd toke one up and choke on our tears
laughing at the glim sunsets in our pupils and
the starry-eyed contradictions of our precious passed time

We'd join the Buddhist circle at Union Square Park
rejoicing in Hare Krishna! Hare Krishna!
Hare Krishna! Hare Krishna!

(I carry your prophetic poems around in jazzy jubilation)

Remember that line you once prescribed?

"...Ah, Carl, while you are not safe I am not safe,
and now you're really in the total animal soup of time."

I wonder too much Ginsy
Are you out there giving the corporate stakeholders
of The Universe a howling lecture
on the fundamentals of eternity?

Your voice vehemently vibrates here on Earth...

You must've finally gone back to that Supermarket in
California
holding Walt's hand the two of you darlings
epically congregating and laughing in the meat section
One can only dare to dream in dystopia

You and I both Ginsy it seems
We're two helpless dreamers stuck in two
not-so-different symphonious American scenes

November 2018
Brooklyn

Don't Worry, About a Thing

I turned to the Internet
Hopped onto YouTube
And began watching a video of
A man signing Bob Marley's
Three Little Birds.
Then he calls a woman up to the mic
To join him in singing. Her voice
Blows the crowd away with a voice of sweet rolling thunder.
The entire crowds is now singing
Don't Worry, About A Thing,
And now everyone's smiling,
And clapping, and being free,
Not worrying about anything.
I shed many tears enjoying
This moment caught on camera
Presented before me in
A worrisome moment, here in the fall of 2020,
Where the human race is engulfed in a global pandemic
Where we must socially distance
Ourselves for one another, for our own safety.
The top YouTube comment said:
This world should be like this....
I long to see that day again and
For the first time

Break Thru and Write

Empty pockets take the weight off my pen.

I release space/time on my own clock

With visions of fellow Writers

composing together and alone.

Our broken wands like bleeding pens

spill out with love our truest of intentions.

We cast a spell and throw out the script.

Our profound words dare one to uplift.

Awakening are our eyes of thought

Into this brisk reality we are taught.

If only for a minute or a millennia

Our voices choke out the gust of mass-hysteria.

The Writer patiently stands still in a stuck line

Holding tightly their hand-constructed lines.

The Writer waits for the bloodshot moon

to carry the weight of their drooling tools

And to spark their tired minds

For times when things aren't fine.

The Writer asks of the power in the soul

to accept these fragmented truths

In order for the words

To break thru

  break thru

   break thru.

For the sacred sanity of I

Yes.

But for more importantly

The blessing that is

and always will be

You.

B38: Downtown Brooklyn to Ridgewood

Inside the heated city bus

around the time school gets out

spare change rolls into the coin slot and

squeaky tires screech at every roadblock.

Teenage boys babble on about the girls

the fights and their social studies homework.

Tails of laughter spill freely from open-wide smiles

and youthful brown eyes.

Toddlers hold on to fun-sized backpacks

as the bus's engine violently hums to their tune

but softly caresses the soles of their golden shoes

and the bottoms of our backs

and the palms of our shivering hands

intertwined in much-needed downtime from

the struggle.

I sit mute

pondering into my people's peaceful commutes

as the window's cracks whisper to me from the left.

Fall is with us rising everyday folk

all silently concerned with our routine rides

thru the vibing streets that make us shine

Indefinitely.

October 2019

The Special Ones Brought

The words BEATI QUI AMBULANT IN LEGE DOMINI
From St. Andrew's Church unknowingly stood before me as
I wrote this

The special ones brought
free water free snacks free juice
free masks free food free chants
free salads free love free quinoa
free cookies free love free hand sanitizer
free love free love free love free love
free signs of freedom signaling a new
yet oddly familiar marching winds of movement
signs that read injustice
anywhere is a threat to justice
everywhere

The special ones brought
their children their students their peers
They brought their tears
They brought their love before their fears
They brought their friends their enemies
their knowledge and their ancestry
ready to be extinguished for those who have fallen
                    their unconditioned souls
            their voices that carry them whole
            they brought their List Of Demands
In the twilight sunlight
poetic spirit of that Saul Williams man

They brought humanity to a standstill
while saying we still have dreams

and their dreams they brought too

and for once that liquid idea
    that their souls were somehow
      sold out
    to a clusterfuck death machine
    of bullets and impunity
dripped from their eyes
and sank into the city sewers
fueling the rats and alligators to join us
in protest of a system we demanded
turn rifles into flowers
and badges into strict oversight
examination

  in exultation

we shout the world soon to be free
and still swallow the fumes
Of our neighbors' day-to-day misery

June 2020
Between New York City Hall & One Police Plaza

The Evens? Or the Odds?

One is the amount of you's there are
And first-and-foremost, it's ok to be odd

Two looks nice

Three is the Holy Trinity
A semblance of fortified balances & checks

Four looks a tad nicer

Five is typically the amount of fingers you own per hand
Use them to build, create, high five or hold your loved ones

Six is an upside down Nine

Seven is lucky–End of story

Eight is supposedly great, but try turning it sideways

Nine is doing fine with its magical ways

Zero is even, according to the mathematicians, therefore
I say we should trust them, because
Zero is also nothing, and
We are looking for something...

So let me ask you: why did you and I
always prefer the evens before the odds?

We aren't born into or even
born onto an even square

We are born into an odd sphere and
born onto an odd sphere

We are unique and organic
And we flow

With the movement
Of the leaves in the wind

Wake-Up Call

Tsunamis came for me in two dreams last evening

There's this unimaginable headrush when you
first realize mountain-sized waves
Towering over clouds & moving faster than a jet plane
are coming at you from all directions

You're stranded and alone
Fucked-out-of-luck
Face-to-face with fate

I'm reluctant to call these waves nightmarish or
believe they belong to some divine vision
or great warning

No matter the speed or height of the wave
I wake before my head is underwater

I prefer to acknowledge them as wake-up calls

Occupation

how does time occupy itself
behind closed doors
where possibility is hushed
inside sealed compartments
where dust collects only memories or dreams of freedom
below the ground roots in bunkers
where the sun never shines nor rests
above the soil in bubbles
where questions about oil are raised
but never answered
inside prison walls
where no one can hear you think
time sits high up on a forgotten shelf
waiting impatiently like the blink of an eye
or like a hospital patient
on care that is not coming
time carefully plots to pierce
the world and rid it of its
unruly congested rotting cages
occupied by the restless minds
begging to be freed of containment

Riding Low

A young day masks the dread

Clouds cry overhead

Heavy sirens roar // Forget the rain

Merely plunges the poor

Get on that train

OK all aboard the Downtown 4

Watch as the passengers

choose to ignore

This little girl selling Oreos

My favorite when I was that young

She asks who wants // Silence crumbles

like forgotten cookie crumbs

Small brown eyes

now carry disdain

She throws down her boxes

Her youth quietly wanes

Unfair this life is when you

Bear witness to the stinging sting

All we can do is try to survive

Or ultimately perish

Deep from within

September 2018
The Bronx

Don't Forget to Float When Lost at Sea

I want you to stay afloat in the daily sea
of a million tired faces riding the endless waves
of trains beneath the city's feet

I used to drown with the flushed out faces too
forgetting to be present in fluid body and soul

Forgetting to smile at stranger fish
even when the water wasn't cold
Forgetting to smile at themselves in the mirror
Forgetting that life sails away fast when you're there
but your attention to the wind's direction isn't
Forgetting to look up and cherish the common drops of rain
The imperfect simpleness of each droplet
the lightness in their laughter
the comfort in their calmness
Forgetting to absorb the love potion
Forgetting to take a break from the Internet
and the endless news cycles
and the daily catastrophes
and the death and disease
and the orderly disorder
and from the thinking
and from the sleeping
Forgetting to inhale and exhale patiently
Forgetting to count blessings even if it's only on two fingers
Forgetting human kindness is always amongst us
Forgetting human forgiveness is beautiful when you give it
a chance
Forgetting past and future pain
Forgetting to let go of the wronging

and to hold on to the longing
Forgetting who you are and
what you desire in this deep sea of games
Forgetting what you wanted to be
& who you are still becoming
Forgetting you hold the keys
even when you feel the water slowly coming
and racing up your lungs but settling in the stiffness
Maybe those faces lost at sea were never held tightly
Or maybe they forgot how to doggy paddle without floaties
and were told as children not to remember
how to navigate unforgiving bodies of water
and in return forgot to care for the bodies of themselves

Breathe in and drink the air

I used to forget to hydrate
when I was down out and blue
But I've since gone fishing on a motorboat
Leaving behind my worries
fingers dripping
hoping to find my next rescue and save you
from the drowning too

On a Subway in Manhattan
July 2019

What Moves You?

A vicious train on a violent track?

A suitcase filled with crisp bills?

A child wondering where his next meal is?

A mother begging for crumbs?

A radio track that hits?

A humming car going ninety?

A fleeting gut-feeling?

An emergency you can't escape?

A vision of endless sunsets?

A pack of green cigarettes?

A prescription designed to have you collapse?

A funny feeling in your unamused bones?

A kitchen knife slicing onions alone at home?

A jolt of thunder in her earthquaking eyes?

A suited man walking in the disguise of his net worth?

An empty, leafless, bookshelf?

Where did those paperbacks ever run off to?

A beggar looking for protein and smokes?

A dying plant? A newborn ant?

Another useless rant?

A protest you watch from the sidelines?

What moves you to keep asking questions

When the answers never seem to rise above sea-level?

The question of being here does

Eat Run Play

A full-bellied toddler
Connected to his mother's leash
Surfaces the city's pavement
Sunny walk on twenty-third street

A forgotten black man
Lay beside the boy's wobbly feet
A paper cup glued to his hand
On the shaded side of concrete

Twenty toes in sight
Two feet they stand apart
Ten starting out on light
Ten peeling in the dark

On the boy's little shirt
It says EAT RUN PLAY
Old man with no shirt
Was life ever just a game?

Ben C. Ward

Following debilitating heartbreak and the end of abusive familial relationships, eighteen-year-old Ben C. Ward began on a journey of self-discovery through poetry. He focuses on the subjects of individuality, time, family, love, depression, nature, and, when he's feeling particularly adventurous, politics. Ward also designed and created the cover for this anthology. Follow him on Instagram for updates on his upcoming debut collection.

You can find him at:

Instagram: @bencwardpoetry
Email: bencwardpoetry@gmail.com

Memento Mori

The city is on fire in the distance, raging reds race up the walls, oranges scorching the skyscrapers and leaving nothing behind. I never had enough time to get there. The air is no longer alone; smoke covers it like a pillow over the face.

I can't find my father's bones, but it's possible that they're mine too. I shudder at the thought and approach the city's edge, where the violin cries broken sobs, trying to catch its breath. Trying to catch my breath. I wear the scars bestowed upon me for my good faith, for my unceasing submission. Batter up!

I have my grandfather's face and I wear it with skill when I'm lying awake at night in the dark. Myrtle trees are outside my window, shining in the sun. But now they die before my eyes, bowing on their knees for the fire. Finality is beginning to feel a lot like childhood.

I find my skull outside my apartment building and stare down the empty eye sockets, as if something will look back at me. My eyes dart to the ruined church, then quickly turn back. I set the skull down hard and keep walking down the street.

I am begging to be touched, ever so slowly, thoughtfully, mournfully. Instead, I come across an assault rifle in the street, smoke crawling desperately from the umbilical cord of a barrel, a full clip next to the gun. There is only ever one question in the world, but I will not ask it here, for the answer has been burned in the fire.

The black clouds look like wings parting in the sky, feathers extending themselves past their welcome. There is silence here, in the center of the city, and I feel overwhelmed with light. The past is a sharp blade forged in a broken fire. Ash decorates the city square, littered in heaps. I don't know what season it is anymore. I don't know what day it is, but maybe it's time.

It's all so hyperreal and I don't know how much longer I can believe in stories. Glass crunches under my feet, painless, yet edged and stark. I stand still, but I am not complacent. I should have been smart enough to take the train, the one nearest the cemetery. Maybe I will find the rest of myself there. Before I can leave, the clouds crackle with impatience, and lightning strikes, calling my name.

Gods of the Road

If this weren't freedom,
then how is it possible that
the direction of the road
follows where my car leads?

The turnpike is where
we learned our limitations,
our faults; we brake far too

soon or so early the sun and
moon tightly embrace behind
the clouds in the morning.

We step in the holes
our fathers never
prepared us for as we fade
to stardust, speeding down
the backroads, giving up our souls

vigorously like the eager
waves that crash on
the old stones of Charleston's walls
or the cocaine beaches
of the Californian coast.

All the while your
hair is infiltrated by the
beautifully relentless wind,
the song of the trees.

Your car is a hybrid,

as deathly quiet as
the chill that sprints up

my spine with a cigarette
in its mouth, poignantly
pouncing on that beam of
starlight that rests inside
your baby blues because

That's where I need
to reside someday. Each
drop of crystalline rain
strums its violin in smooth
union,

not broken like the serpentine
cracks in the road, filled with
the blood we take for granted

as fall's infancy arrives,
springing from summer's
womb, leaves of dying colors fall,
with no inkling
of the war that waits.

Moonrise

Craters litter the field.
I can't understand
if the bombs
rest here or if
they're just dead
dreams.

Subtlety
has been lost
on me
but the protest
still flows
solemnly along the banks
of those creeks buried
deep in the highlands
with the skeletons
of the red,
the white,
the blue.
The careless
colonialists,
the impaired imperialists.

Fear
is now a lexicon;
maybe it's been hiding
under the guise
of hunger.
Orange wraps her slick
and omnipotent hands
around the threats

of unsuspecting trees
and the lungs of
my brothers-in-arms.
streaked by error,
clothed in screams,
silence is but a season.
Move in,
go ahead,
raise the barrel
and maybe you'll be safe.

Fire your gun.
How else
can you feel
secure?

Never, ever surrender.
How could I?

Freedom is dimming
but she still
holds her ground.

Rain crawls up at me,
devotion calling
faintly from the heavens.

There are none to be found,
so make damn sure
your body count
is on

Target.

Point.
Aim.
Shoot.
The trigger
is a thing of the

present.
It pierces
with cold
defiance.

Silhouettes don't
bleed, so take it
easy and don't
let them see.
Red pollutes
my shadow,
making him
reckless
with clarity.

Huey's making
his way into
the July sky,
carrying his
children from
the furnace.

Charlie is
tiptoeing
in the forest,
looking up,
looking around.

Ben C. Ward

Here I am,
anxious for the
grenade
to make its debut.

The men fall like
blades of grass
during a lawnmower
massacre
in the suburbs
on a Sunday.

The trail snakes
like paint escaping the brush,
leaving generations in its wake.

Love Song From the Edge of the Planet

Stars reverberate off of the walls with displeasure.
    angry at me, or maybe it's just jealousy.

The bruises left on the earth's skin harken back to a
    time where I bled profusely in waiting.

A glass half empty is less than a glass half full.

The ocean falls in and sinks at the sight of you,
    at the night of you.

We dance courageously atop the mountain's fingers,
    high above the autumn and her children,

Indistinguishable from a summer storm, barraging the
    secrets ruthlessly. Nowhere to hide,

Everywhere to be seen. My home is somewhere in the mist,
    yours is in between the blades of grass

Outside the dark but not quite in the grey. I suppose if
    the diamonds cried, the streetlights would

Call out for you, like I am right now. I never needed a
    reason to love you. I just needed a word:

You. I'm burning alive in my glass box as the brakes grind
    to a halt. Metal on bone, heart to heart.

Collapse is anything but imminent. Even so, you break
    the barrier like a hurricane falling facedown

Into the arms of his mother. Distance is much like the
    morgue, but we don't belong to a body bag.

Fragments are keys just waiting to be played and I can't
    help but cave at the ends of your sentences.

Three words, proof that maybe less is indeed more. Sun
    touches the tips of your hair, igniting

Devotion, a temple made flesh, smooth as paper lips,
    unlocking the door to a boundless universe.

The seasons call, but you don't come to the door, for you
are in all of them.

A 3 A.M. Crime Scene

I don't know if I chose the void of fire.
I don't know if I said yes to being carved
from the inside out like a pumpkin,
the mountain of guts next to my corpse,
so I was pretty and hollow enough
for his liking.

I held myself together with nothing
but an outline drawn in white chalk.
I shiver and black out. Will I remember
my future?

It was hunger and nothing more. It did not
belong to me. I know I shouldn't but
I jealously wish that I were the night sky.

I am a collage pieced together by a clueless artist.
I bury my face in the pillow and I see stars.
God, it's 4:37 now, and I need to sleep, but
my favorite song just came on.

Mesmerized

For Kennedy

The room smells like you, so I write in my journal.
Beneath our blanket, I stare and wonder if there is a
connection between your eyes
and the ocean's pale skin during winter.

I do not know if I will find the answers I seek, for they
lay tucked away inside a dusty cardboard box in a
closet at the end of this long hallway.

My hands are fiercely staining with red, though that
is better than doing nothing at all. But there is a
book, one that I hope is enough when I read it to you.

The coroner has finished the autopsy, determining
the cause of death. The poet has finished the poem,
determining the cause of loving.

I'll count your freckles like a child counts clouds in the sky,
sitting on the plane, racing against time. My heart will
always beat faster, my pen going up in flames when
you put your hand to mine.

Ink and Blood

I was the only one coming,
       later than I was supposed to

as I broke the air open with
       a finger crafted from ink

and blood. I didn't think much
       about what it meant

to drown but I knew what it was
       to kneel, to pledge

with my flimsy glory and blond
       curls. I emerged from a

tsunami on the backs of white
       poppies. There was so much

more than the sterile, broken-hearted
       limbs I would soon

know, as familiar as the bones
       nailed together to birth

a shelf. I was worth my weight in
       words, a product of two

meandering sentences.

I colored with blue but always
       strayed away

from the tombstones.

The eraser knew who I was
        long before I did,

writing in seasons, speaking in mirrors,
        loving in roads, teaching

in standstills.

Once, I Stood in Front of the Water Lilies

For Kennedy

A ribcage punctures the heart
      on a sea of white ripples.

An ocean of red falls on its back
      in the middle of the grocery store

where nobody but you can see. I held
      infinity close to my chest without

really knowing what that meant. My eyes
      closed and I could feel the war

on the outskirts of the city, far from
      the lilies. But not for long.

I was bewildered to find a gaping hole
      that didn't stare at me with pity.

October drifts through the oaks,
      the wind the silvery-blue color of your eyes.

stealing what little breath I have left. The road
      seems so far away from the airplane

and yet I feel like a stray lightning bolt
      frantically grasping at the shards

on the ground with all the care in the world.
      Feeling a bit hazy, I took a walk.

I heard a gunshot, then remembered where I live.
    The war here hides behind French doors

and freshly mowed lawns, courtesy
    of the boy who lives just down the road.

Toward the end of my walk, I got a little lost,
    made my way away from the battlefield.

Footsteps imprinted among the falling ash and ruin
    while I kept my mind fixated on that voice

that could give a happy ending to the monumental
    silence. The world was at war

and as my foot broke the wave, I looked forward
    and saw the breeze weave through your hair.

I was witness to an ethereal presence. Yours. You.

You, in your Claude Monet shirt with the water lilies.
    You, who held me in the still darkness

when the clock was on the brink of midnight.

Our Last Words

The stars are bullet holes in the night sky
as I graduate from being alone to being alone again.
My eyes are shut on a cool summer evening
in this godforsaken town, when I stand under the full moon,
pleading for a respite from the broken clock.
I walk past six anthills, each one bigger than the last
and I wonder how it can be possible to build up instead
of tearing down.
There is no garden, because who would tend it?
Gravel crunches like bones beneath my shoes, the dust rolls
behind me like tear gas. Like the others, I was frozen
by the future, a deer in the oncoming headlights.
Melancholy digs an unmarked grave, stark raving mad.
Under pressure, she claims to be a staunch monogamist.
Maybe she said conservative and I just need to get my damn
ears checked out by the local pediatrician.
Maybe I'm just hearing what I want to hear,
under the sturdy oak that has dominion over the front yard,
dying piece by piece as I go back and forth on the
homemade swing. What is keeping me from falling?
I look at all the books on the shelf and try to determine
how many years I have left in me.
There is more than the pasture, but I only discovered
the truth because I opened my cheap coffin for a peek.
I saw the steeple of a Baptist church.
I saw the road.
I saw a choice. I made it.
For some time, I dreamt of New York City.
Walt Whitman and the works.
That grid system. Those neighborhoods we all know
but never really truly know.

In the year two thousand and nineteen, I paid my respects
to my past by searching for it in every face I saw.
I looked for brown eyes.
I foraged for Neruda.
I sought after Ginsberg.
I scavenged for Plath.
I held on by the tips of my fingers even as the rain smoothed
down the sides of the city's skyscrapers,
leaving behind only a reflection and a question.
What is the question?
All sensibility seems to have left this town;
the schools are open; the curve is not flattening.
There are exit wounds in my memory, begging the
question of who fired the gun.
I'm sure I can find the right answer from only four choices.
Four is not enough zeroes to buy the vaccine, so add more.
I do not know how to recover what has been lost,
but I imagine if I read enough, I can.
I can.
I can.
I can.
In the year two thousand and twenty, I learned one truth
among the rest.
It took many years of persistent, yearning inquiry, but I was
looking in the clouds far above the earth when I found
the truth amongst the trees, right before me,
as it always was.
If there is a question, then there always is an answer.
Time will end once poetry does, and if poetry falls on the
sword, she will go out uttering a lyric that will go on
long after time exhales its last breath.

ACKNOWLEDGMENTS

As the editor of this anthology, I would like to thank each and every poet in this anthology for their time and effort, through Zoom calls, one-on-one conversations, and their endless support. Every single one of you are bringing new light into the world through your poetry, and your words will not be forgotten.

I would also like to thank Charles Clark and Casey Nissenbaum for their years of support, advice, and friendship. Both of you made me believe in my writing at a critical time.

Many, many thanks to Andy O'Hara and Karen Dinsmore, who provided very helpful assistance and proofreading for this anthology.

I want to thank the ever-so-lovely Kennedy Conrady. Without her, writing seems to be a bland experience. She has a large hand in inspiring me constantly and drives me to be better.

I would be remiss if I didn't thank Robert Cozzi, who has been my friend for years, who I teamed up with for this anthology. It is him I must thank for his thoughtful critiques, meaningful advice, inside jokes, and close friendship. He introduced me to many great people I now call good friends, and I will always be grateful for that.

Finally, I would like to extend my thanks to a beautiful group of people: Jennifer Childress, Terrell Childress, Cheryl Ward, Shane Hudalla, Robin Emery, Angie Horstmeyer,

Wyatt Horstmeyer, Emily Free, Sara Free, Harry Cooper, Alex Adams, John Brown, Toni Brown, Jeremy Studivant, Kirat Randhawa, Lisa Driscoll, Margaret Phillips, Annemarie Biondi, Susan Williams, John Mattox, Sam Pennington, Tyler Vance, Ocean Vuong, David Mack, Paul Kocum, Sanford Greene, Beth Hermes, Debi Merchant, and last but certainly not least, Jim Bryan.

The impact all of these individuals have had on me is truly immeasurable in the grandest sense of the word. Thank you all for the endless inspiration, adventures, and unforgettable experiences. If these experiences were absent from my life, writing poetry would feel incomplete. But, it goes without saying: Poetry must and will live on. It is within us all. We just have to find it.

Ben C. Ward
November 20th, 2020

Made in the USA
Monee, IL
16 June 2021

71533317R00144